Venn That Tune

ABOUT THE AUTHOR:

Andrew Viner has a degree in electronic engineering and only became a writer after picking an evening course at random. He has been a winner of a BBC scriptwriting competition with his radio play *Goal Difference*, and first wrote for Aardman's *Rex the Runt*. He has since written sketches and gags for radio comedy shows and has also written for the *Guardian*. He writes extensively for children's television, including shows such as *Rubbadubbers*, *Bear Behaving Badly* and *Thomas the Tank Engine & Friends*.

Venn That Tune

Andrew Viner

HODDER &
STOUGHTON

First published in Great Britain in 2008 by Hodder & Stoughton
An Hachette Livre UK company

1

Copyright © Andrew Viner 2008

The right of Andrew Viner to be identified as the Author of the Work has been asserted by him in
accordance with the Copyright, Designs and Patents Act 1988.

A CIP catalogue record for this title is available from the British Library

ISBN 978 0340 955673

Printed & bound in Italy by Graphicom

Hodder & Stoughton policy is to use papers that are natural, renewable and recyclable products
and made from wood grown in sustainable forests. The logging and manufacturing processes are
expected to conform to the environmental regulations of the country of origin.

Hodder & Stoughton Ltd
338 Euston Road
London NW1 3BH

www.hodder.co.uk

Introduction

The idea for this book came from the ZZ Top song Gimme All Your Lovin', the chorus of which begins "Gimme all your lovin', all your hugs and kisses too". I could never understand why ZZ Top felt the need to specify hugs and kisses too when they had already said that they wanted "all" lovin'. In the context of a Venn diagram, they were placing hugs and kisses outside the set of lovin' (fig. i).

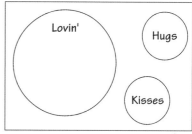

fig. i

Call me a romantic old fool, but I have always felt that hugs and kisses are all part of the lovin', and that it is a tautology to request them separately. My Venn diagram would place hugs and kisses very much inside the set of lovin' (fig. ii).

It is not even as if, like the Spencer Davis Group in 1966, ZZ Top were asking only to be given "some" lovin', which of course might not have included

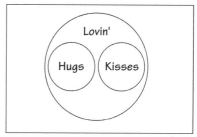

fig. ii

hugs and/or kisses. No, they were asking for "all" lovin', but still felt the need to specify hugs and kisses as extras, as though they were getting their lovin' from a lady of the night who would have additional charges for such things (I would imagine). "Gimme all your lovin' (by which I implicitly include all your hugs and kisses)" may not scan quite so well, but perhaps that is a small price to pay for exactitude.

I never did find out why ZZ Top felt that they had to ask for hugs and kisses too, but it did get me thinking about song titles from the UK Top 40 that I could depict in the form of Venn diagrams or other graphs or charts. So, here is a whole book of them. Answers are at the back.

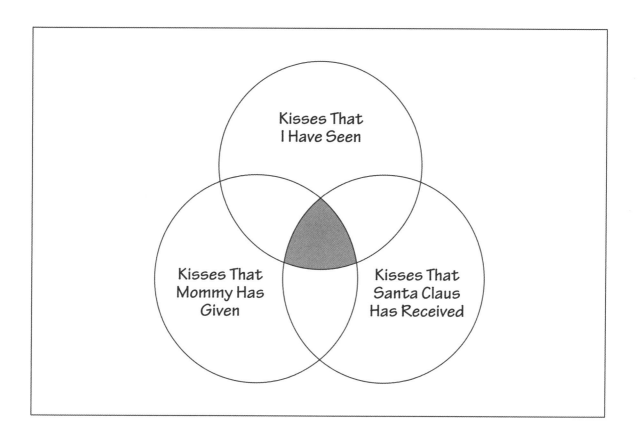

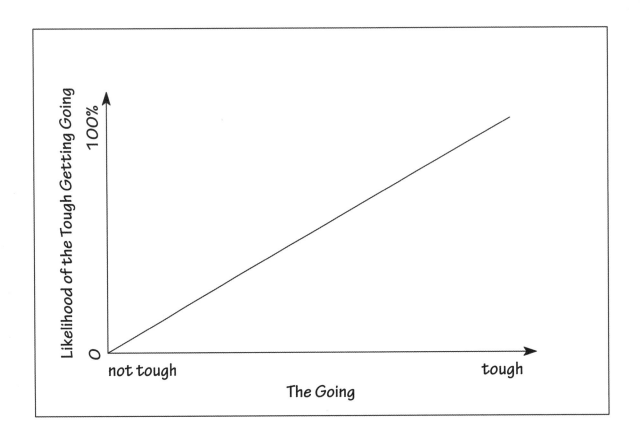

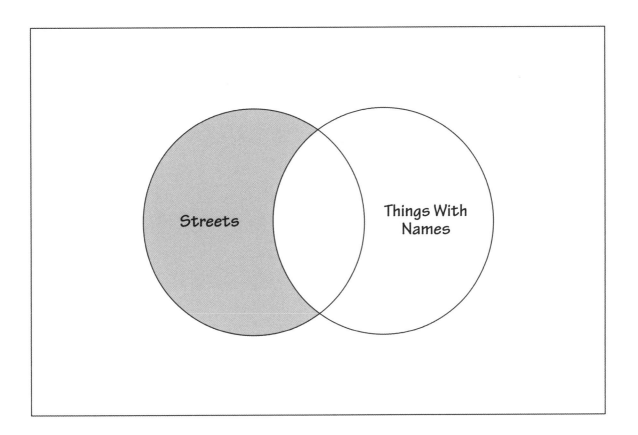

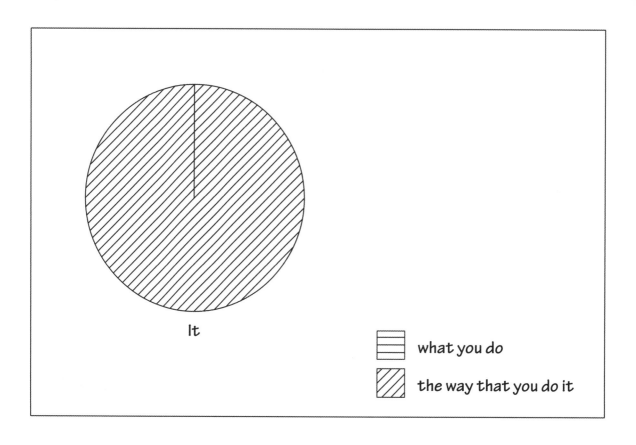

It

what you do

the way that you do it

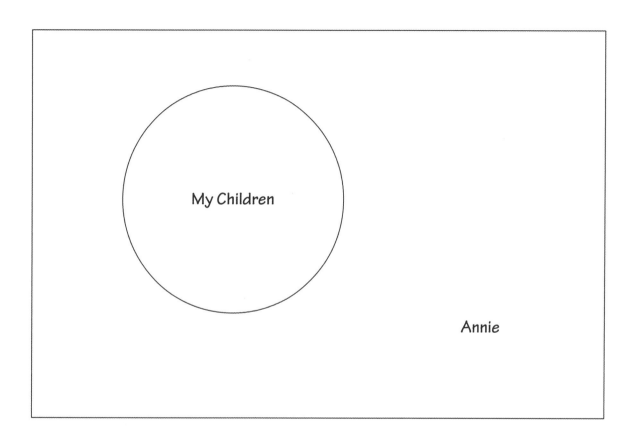

My Children

Annie

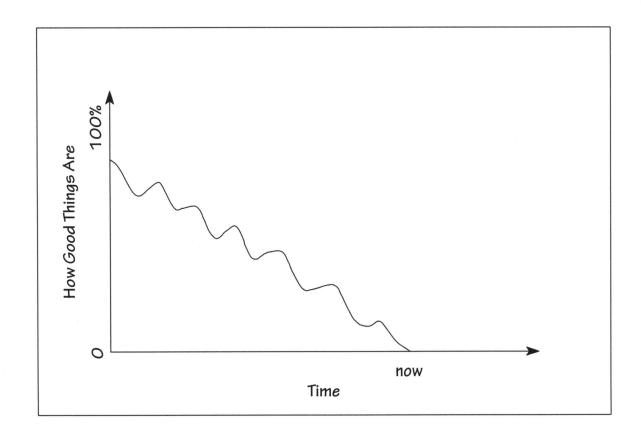

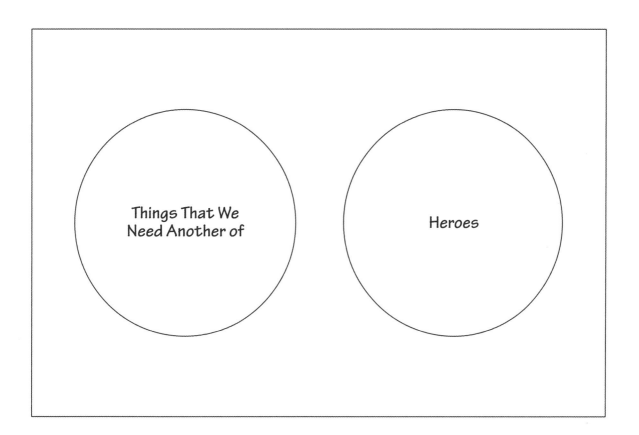

Things That We
Need Another of

Heroes

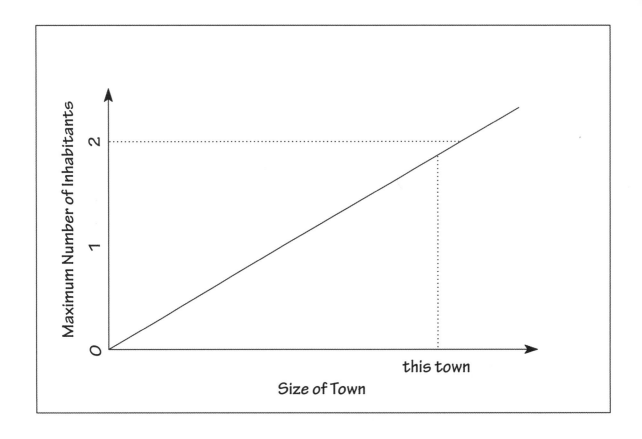

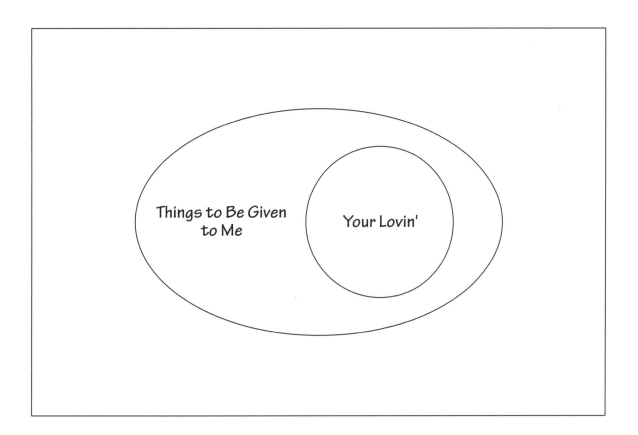

Things to Be Given to Me

Your Lovin'

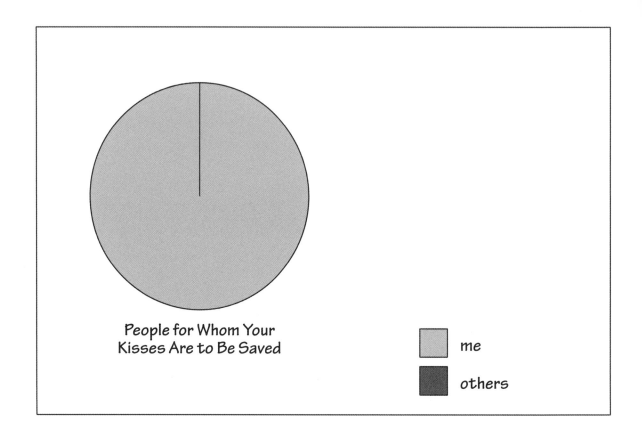

People for Whom Your
Kisses Are to Be Saved

me

others

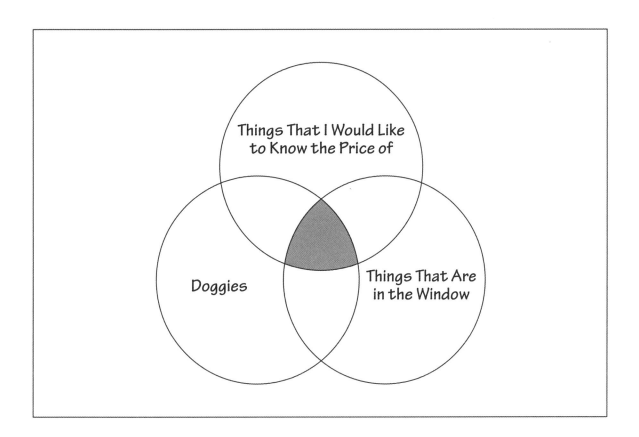

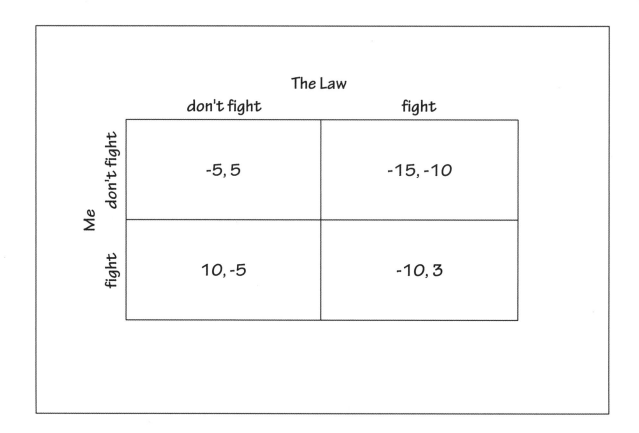

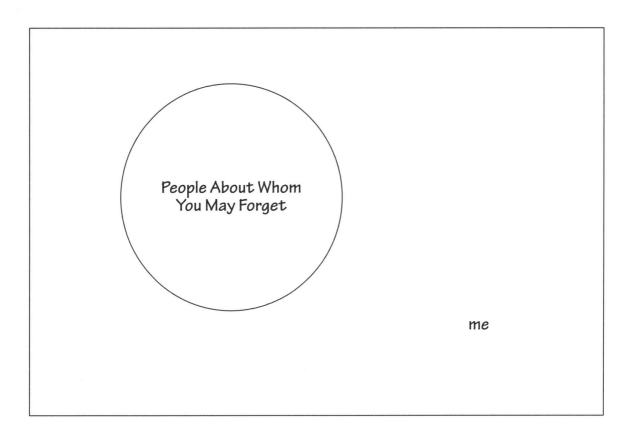

People About Whom
You May Forget

me

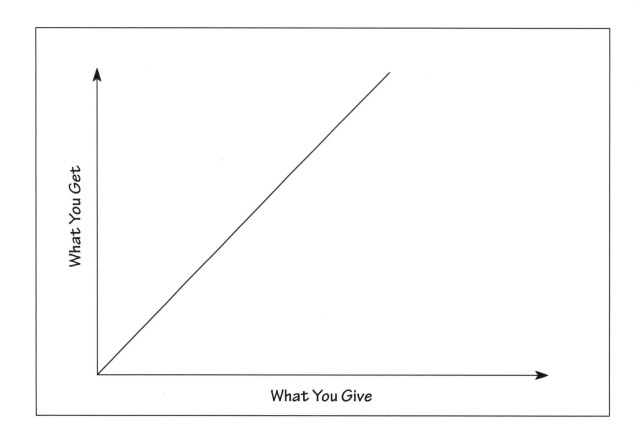

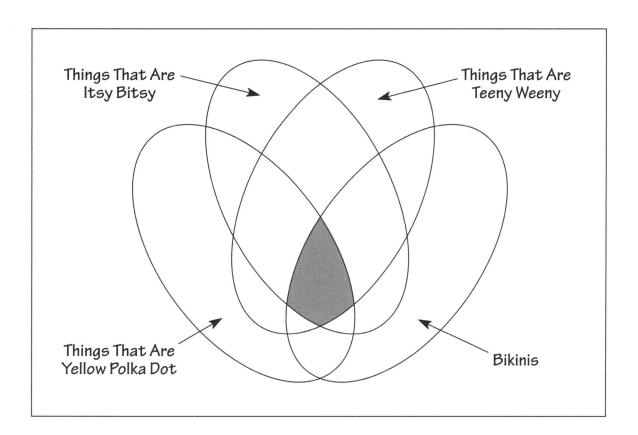

Things That Are
Itsy Bitsy

Things That Are
Teeny Weeny

Things That Are
Yellow Polka Dot

Bikinis

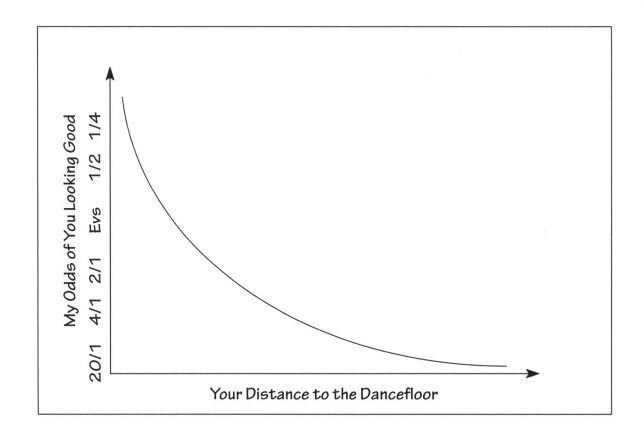

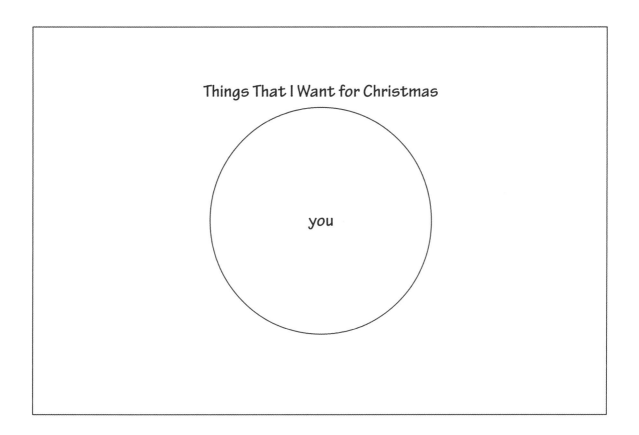

Things That I Want for Christmas

you

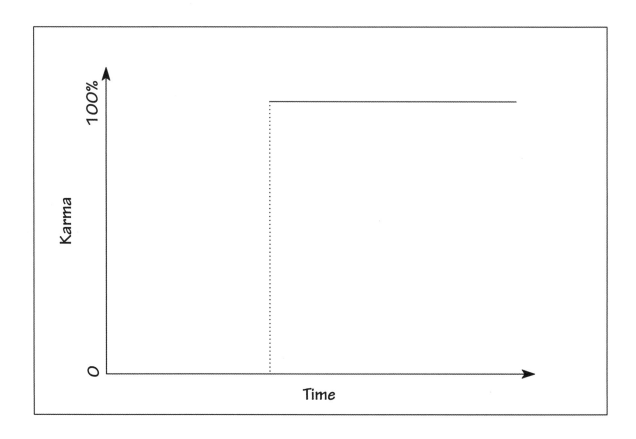

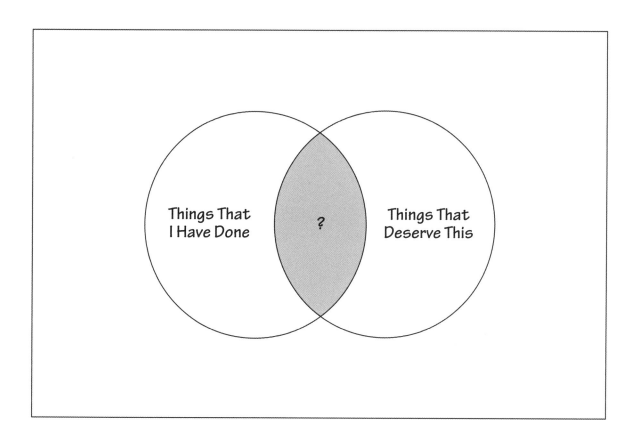

Things That I Have Done

?

Things That Deserve This

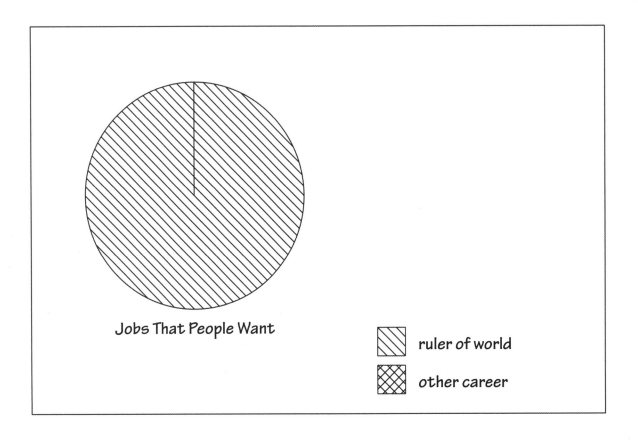

Jobs That People Want

ruler of world

other career

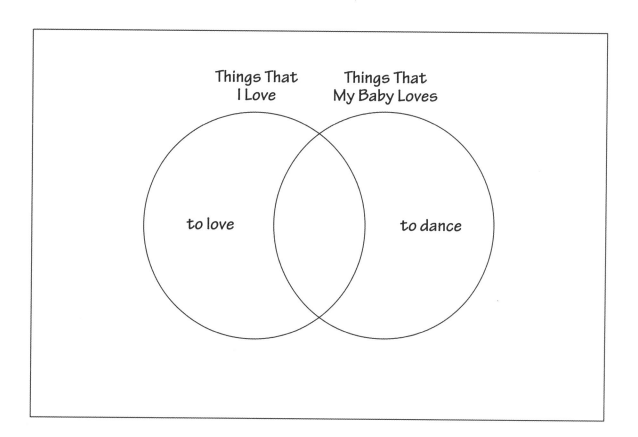

Things That
I Love

Things That
My Baby Loves

to love

to dance

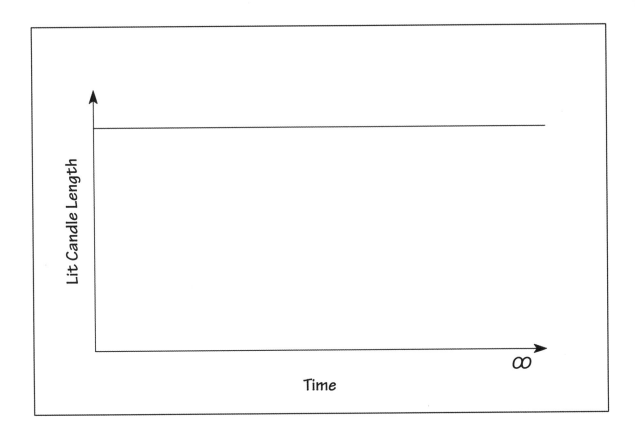

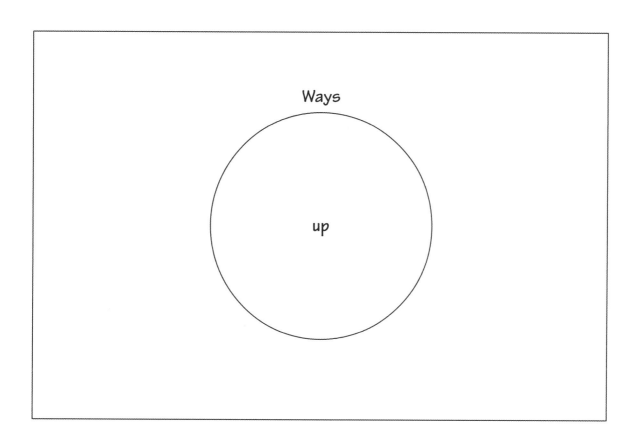

Ways

up

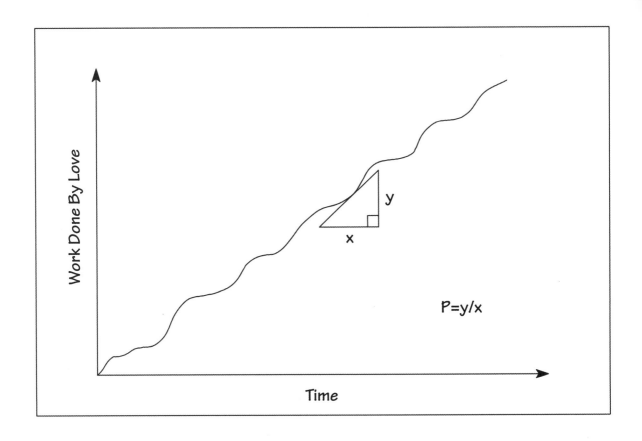

Work Done By Love

Time

$P=y/x$

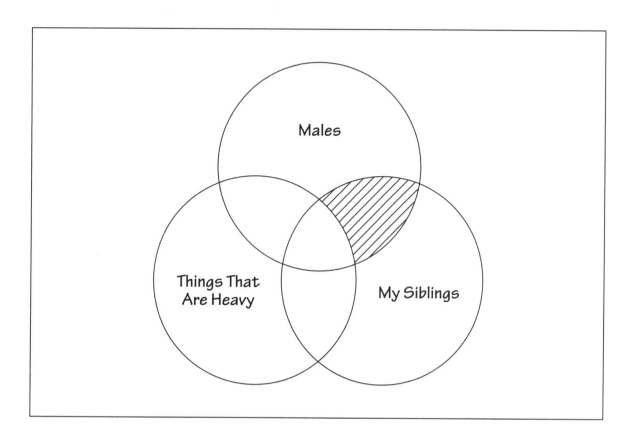

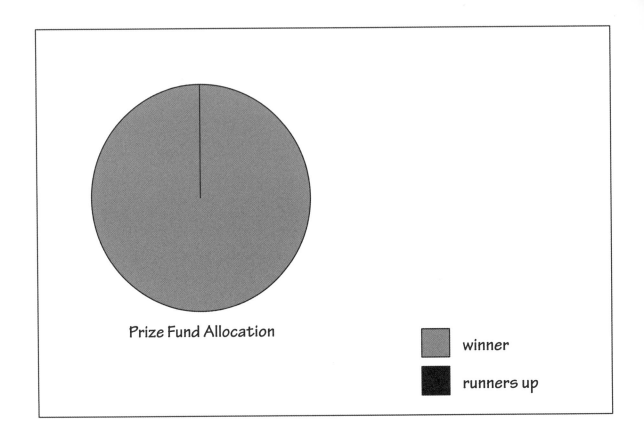

Prize Fund Allocation

winner
runners up

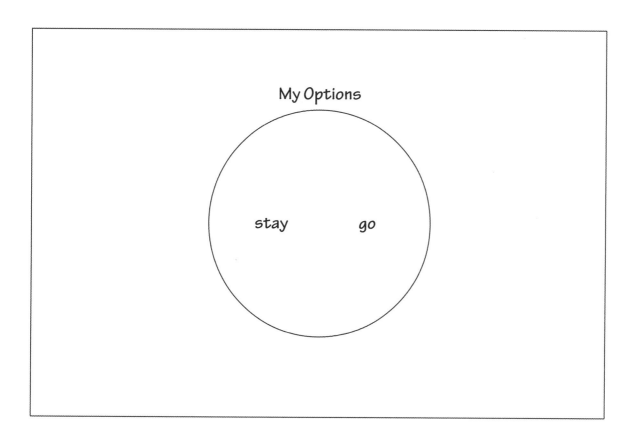

My Options

stay   go

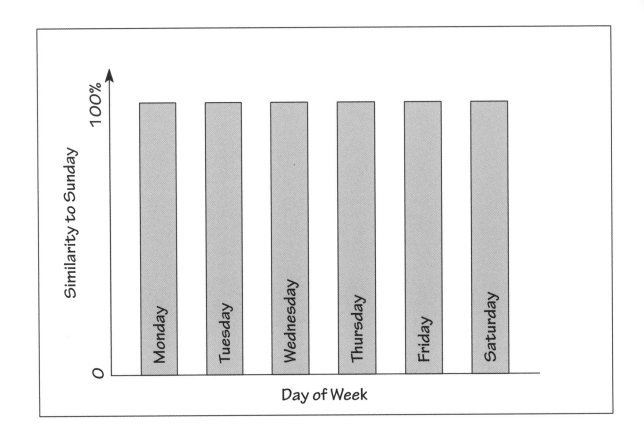

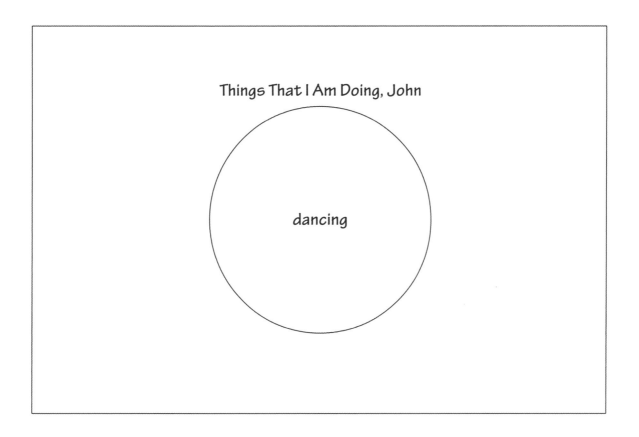

Things That I Am Doing, John

dancing

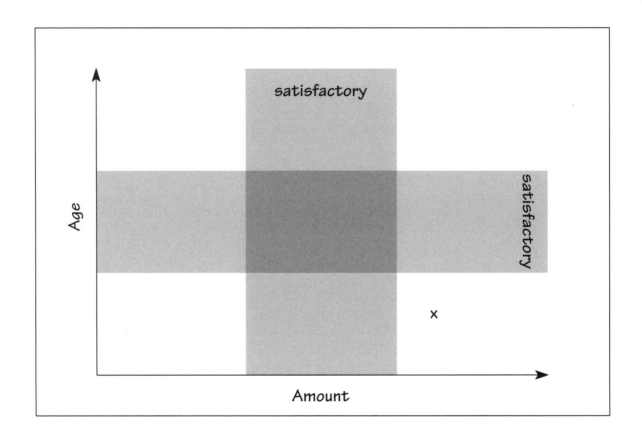

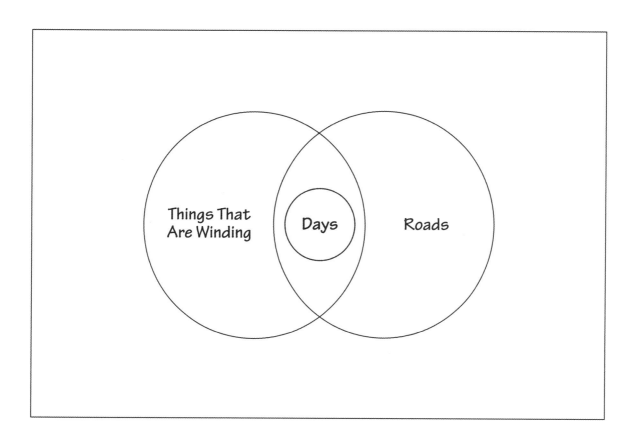

Things That Are Winding

Days

Roads

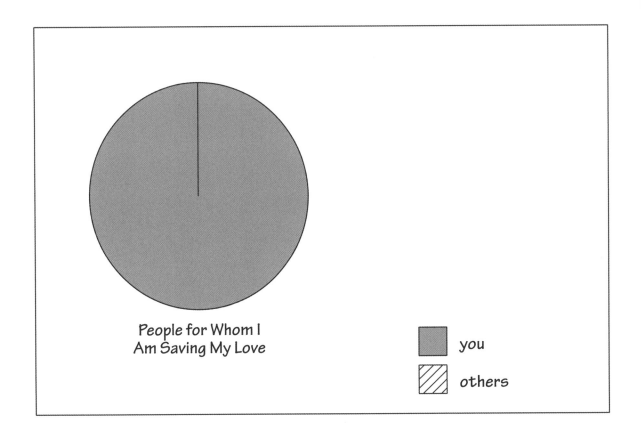

People for Whom I
Am Saving My Love

you

others

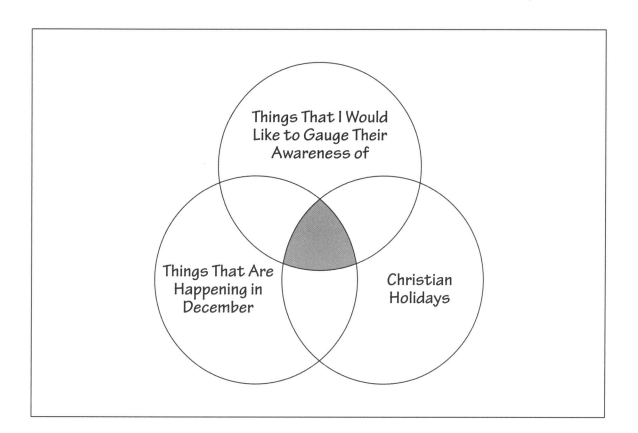

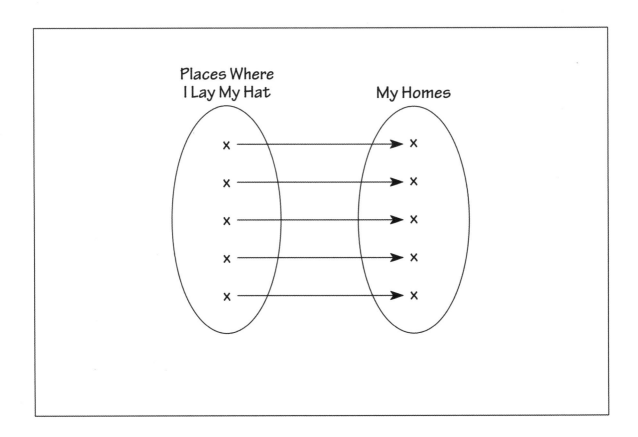

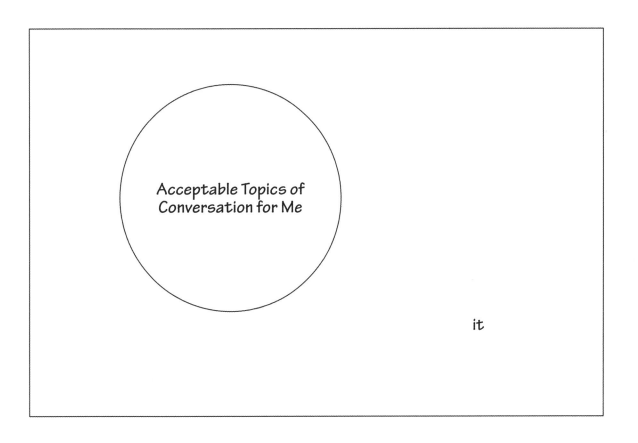

Acceptable Topics of
Conversation for Me

it

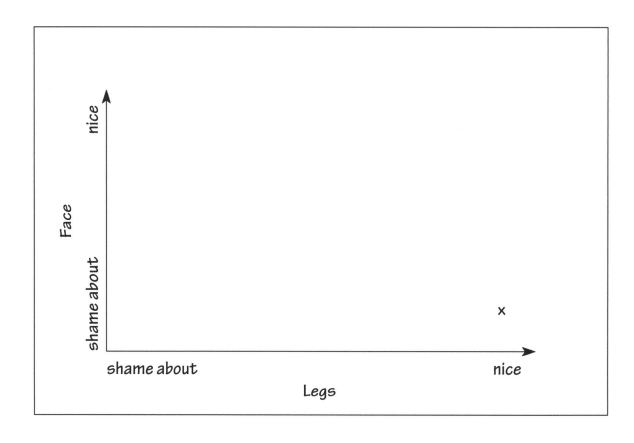

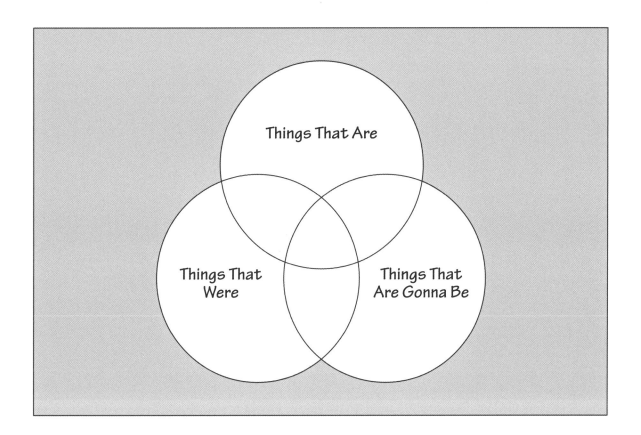

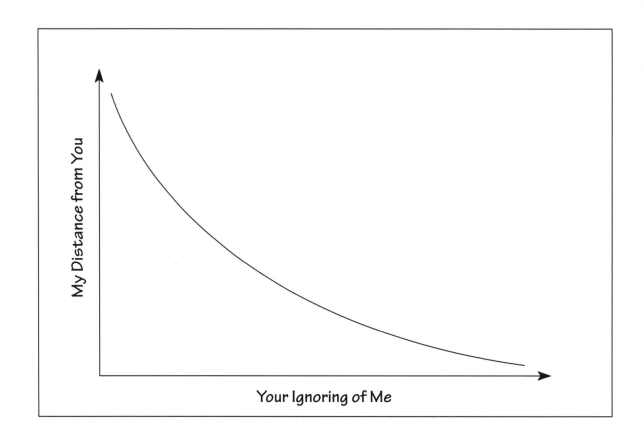

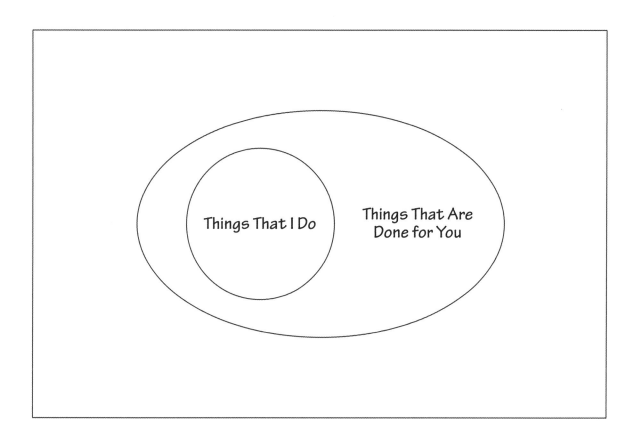

Things That I Do

Things That Are
Done for You

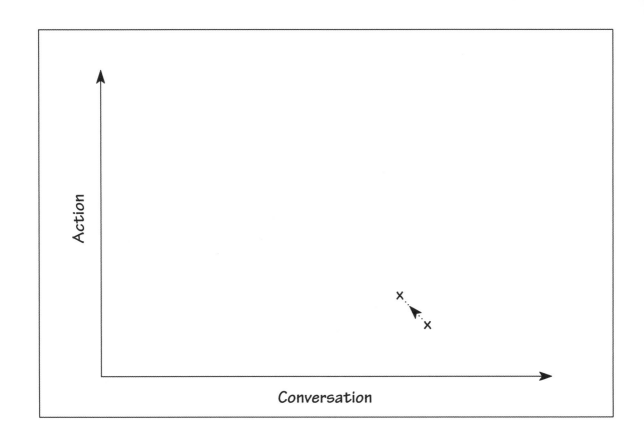

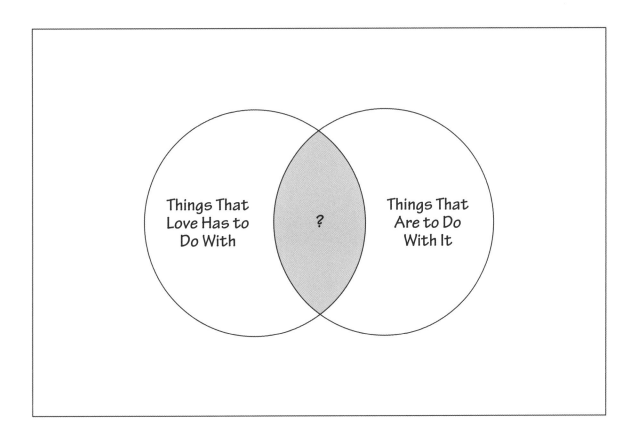

Things That
Love Has to
Do With

?

Things That
Are to Do
With It

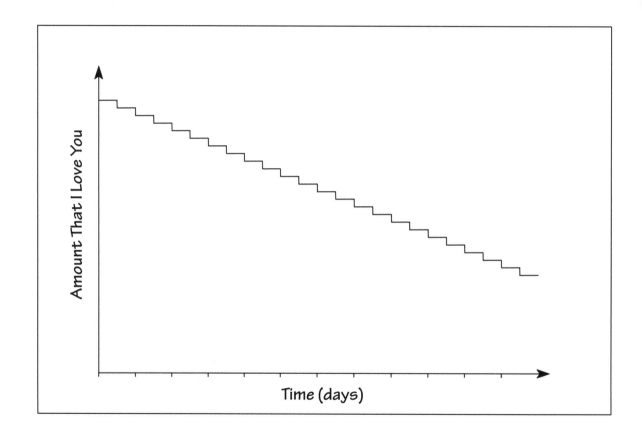

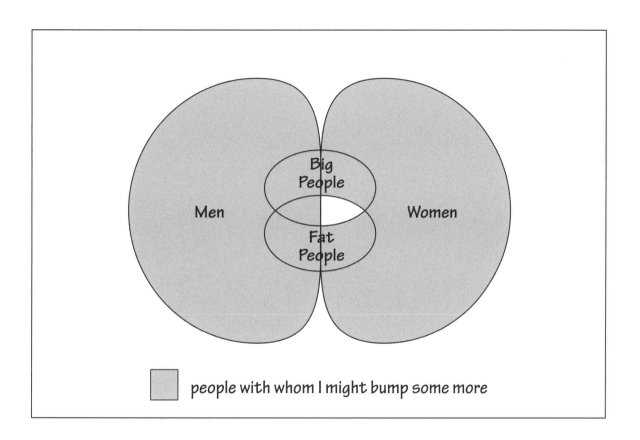

people with whom I might bump some more

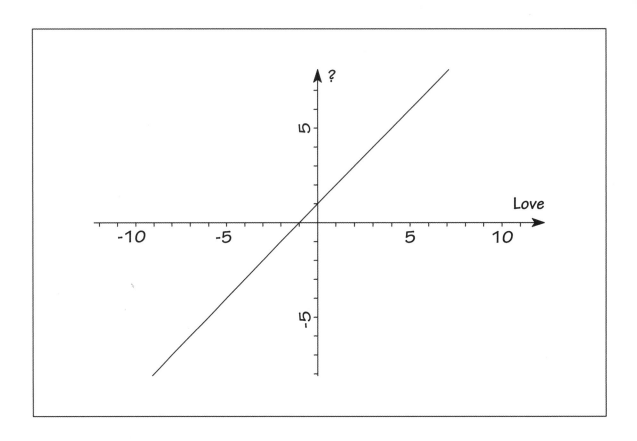

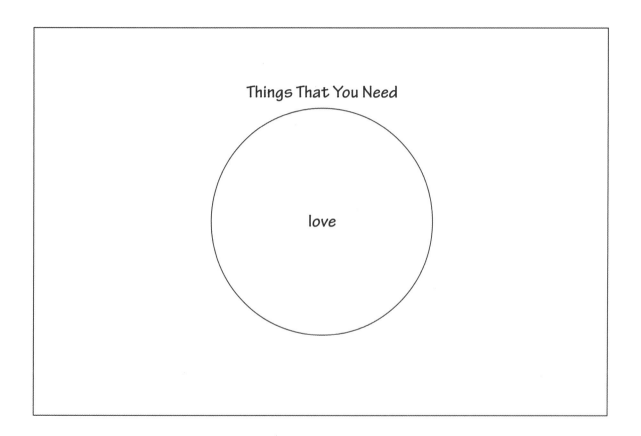

Things That You Need

love

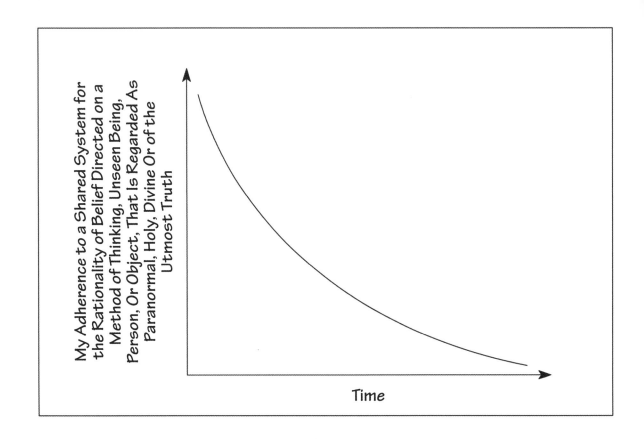

My Adherence to a Shared System for the Rationality of Belief Directed on a Method of Thinking, Unseen Being, Person, Or Object, That Is Regarded As Paranormal, Holy, Divine Or of the Utmost Truth

Time

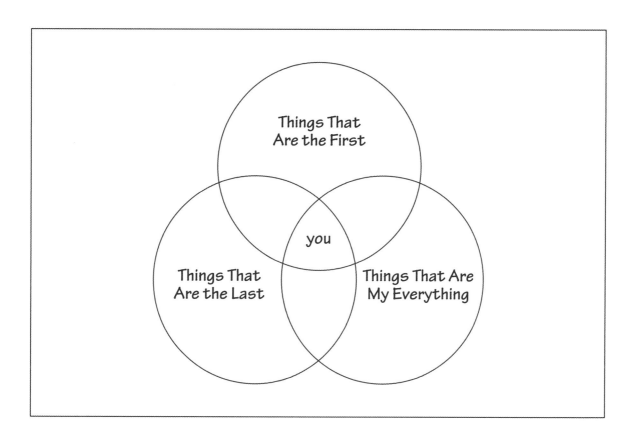

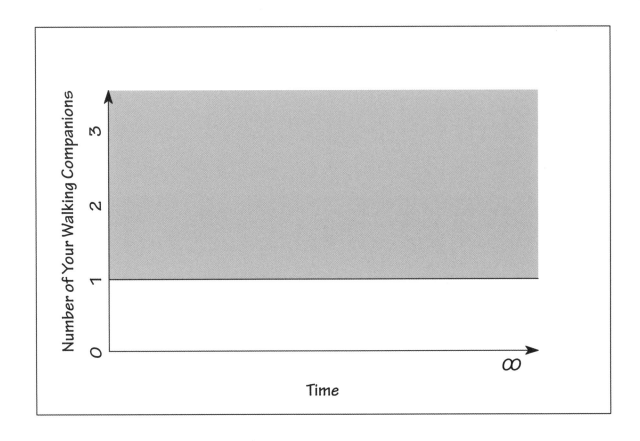

48

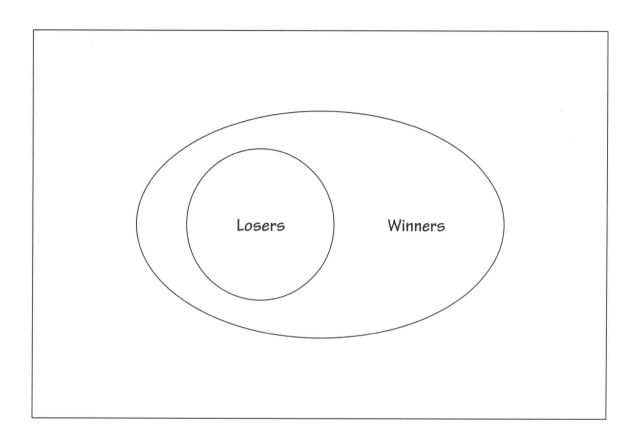

Losers

Winners

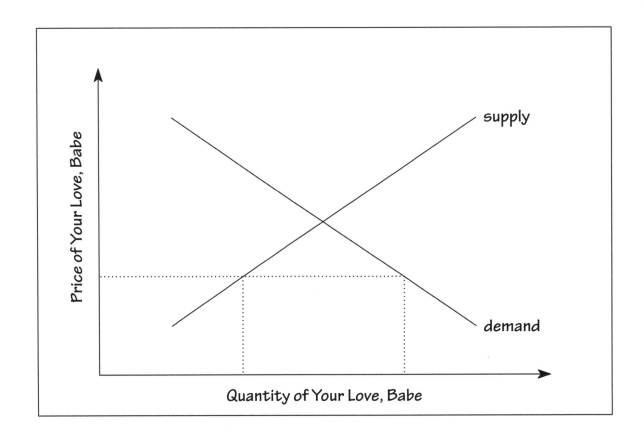

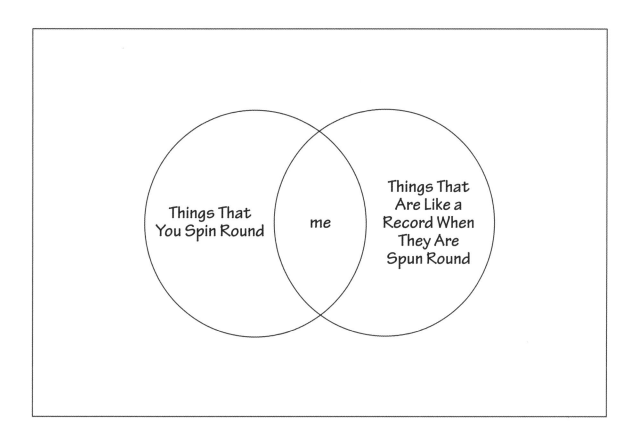

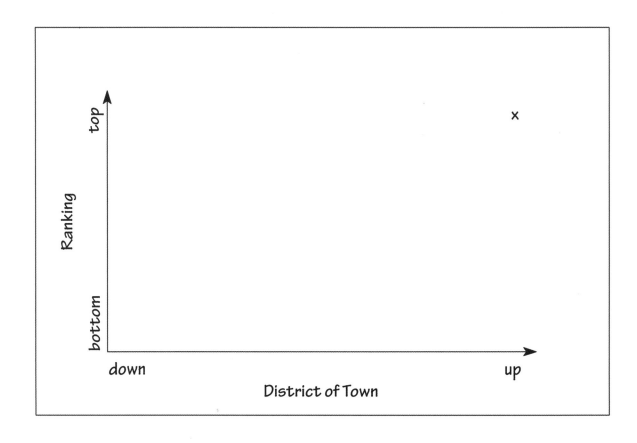

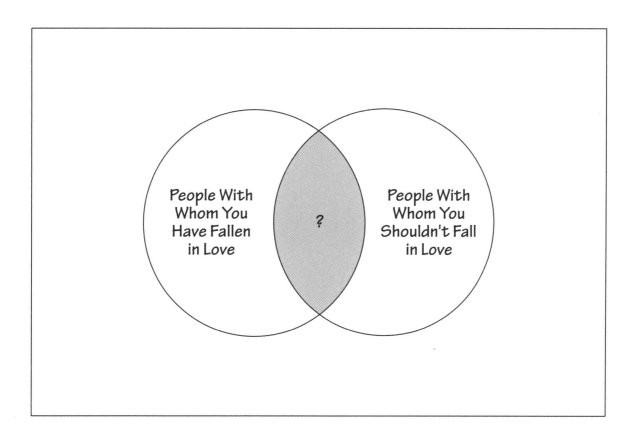

People With Whom You Have Fallen in Love

People With Whom You Shouldn't Fall in Love

?

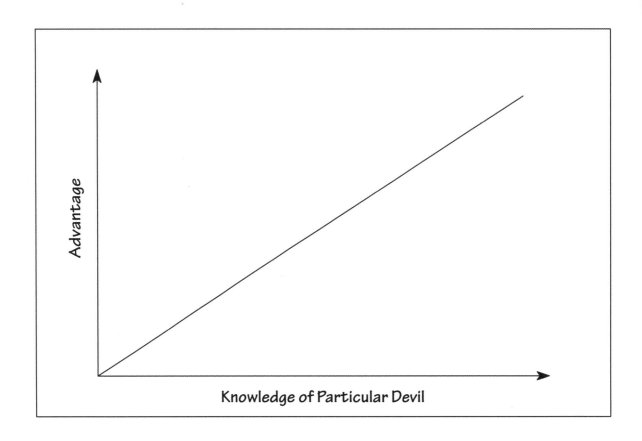

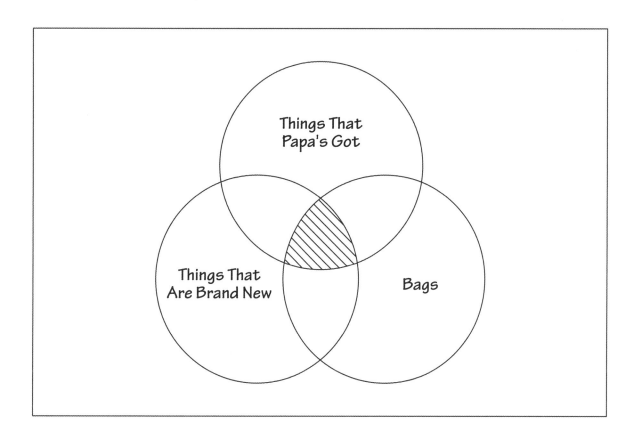

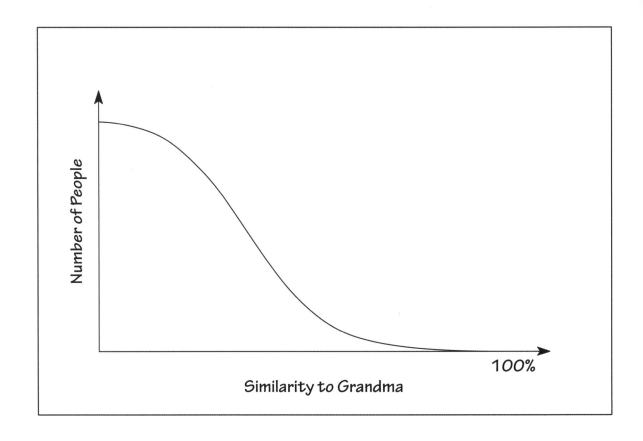

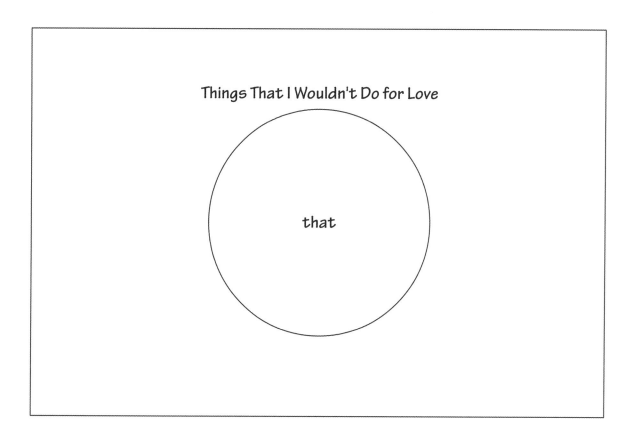

Things That I Wouldn't Do for Love

that

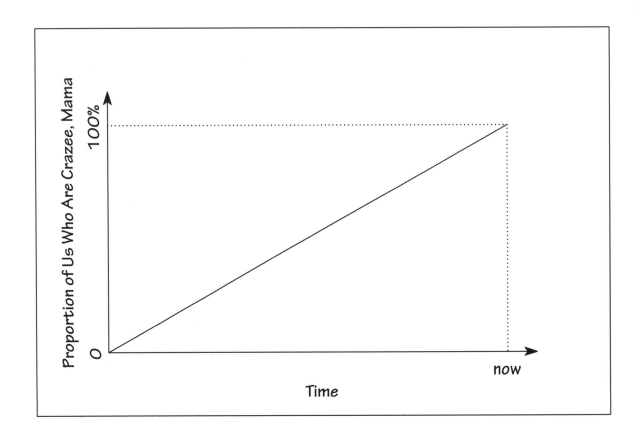

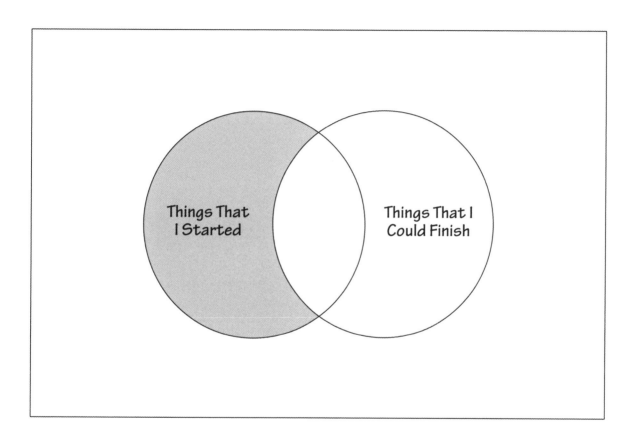

Things That I Started

Things That I Could Finish

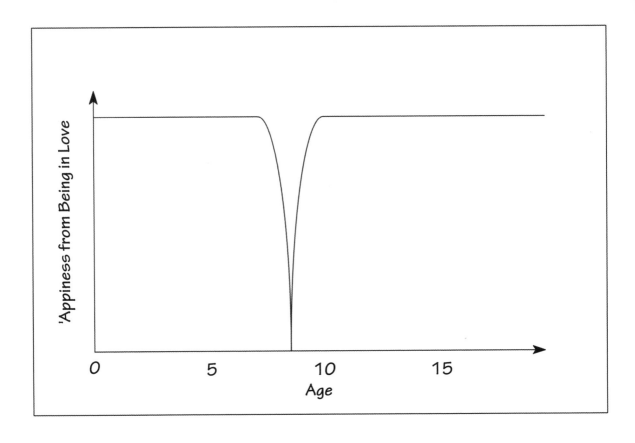

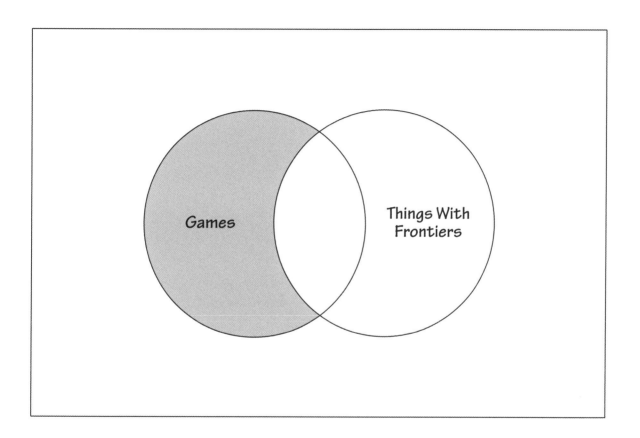

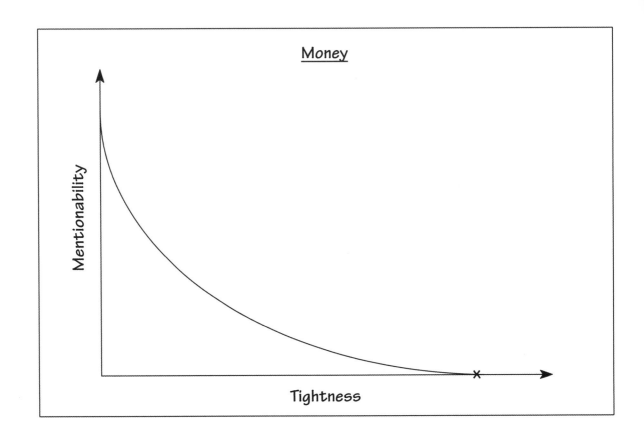

Money

Mentionability

Tightness

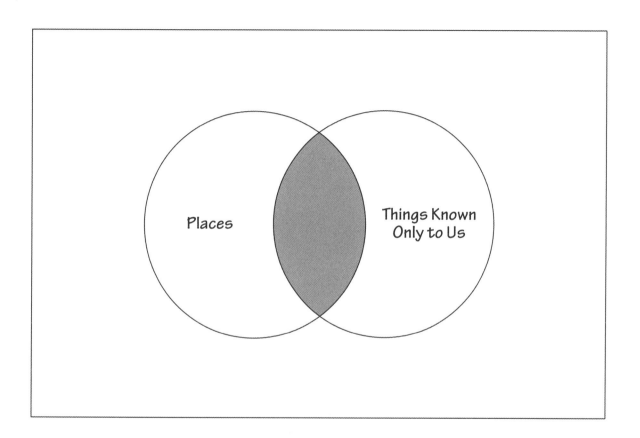

Places — Things Known Only to Us

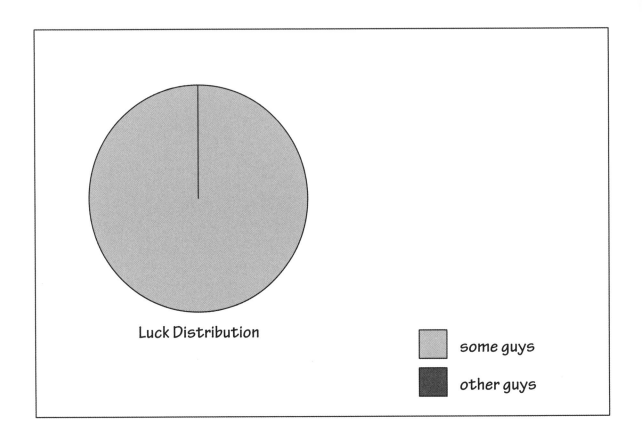

Luck Distribution

some guys

other guys

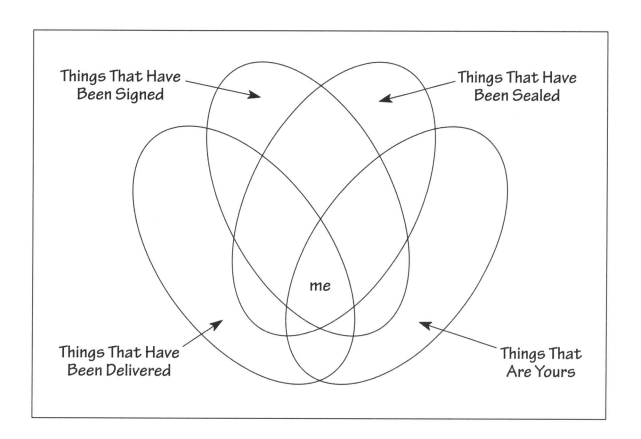

Things That Have Been Signed

Things That Have Been Sealed

Things That Have Been Delivered

Things That Are Yours

me

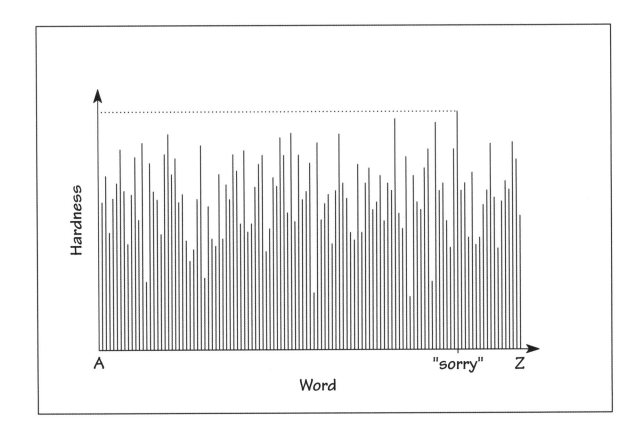

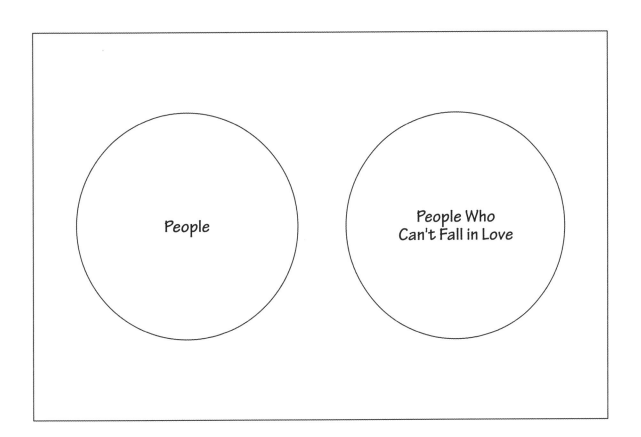

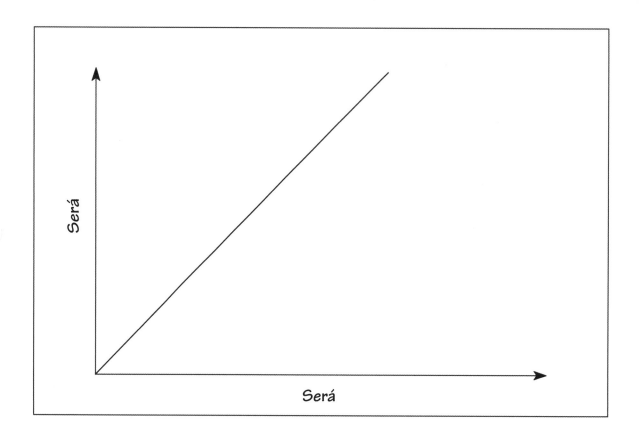

Será

Será

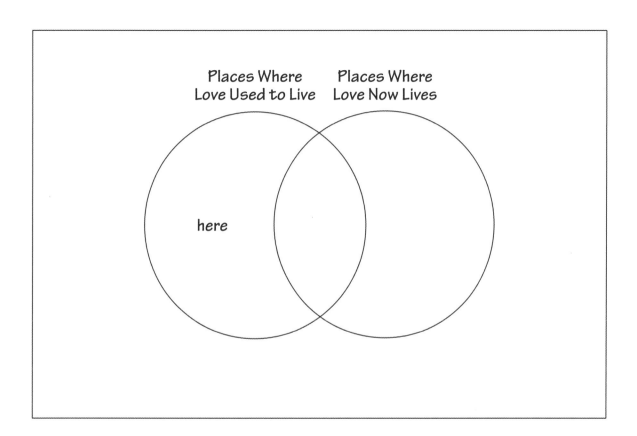

Places Where
Love Used to Live

Places Where
Love Now Lives

here

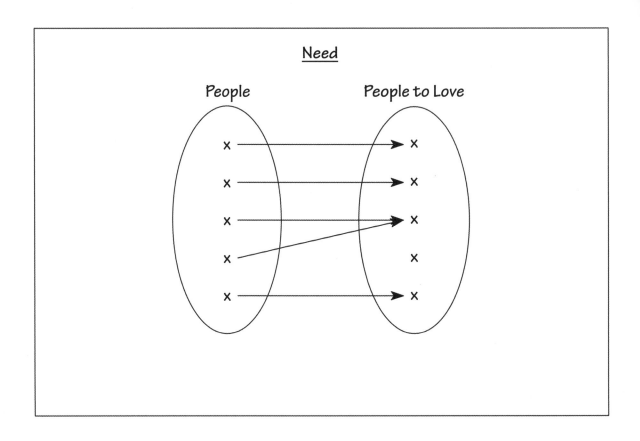

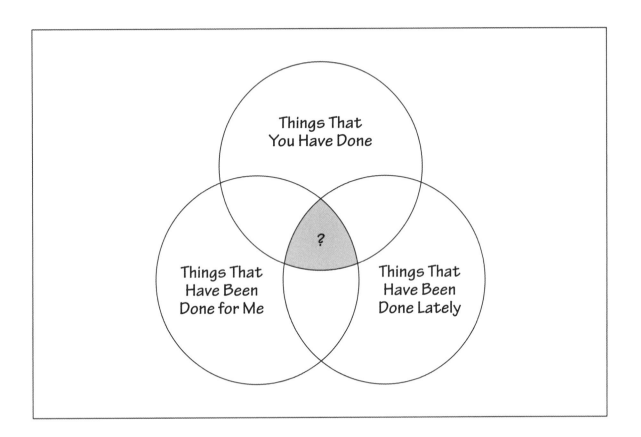

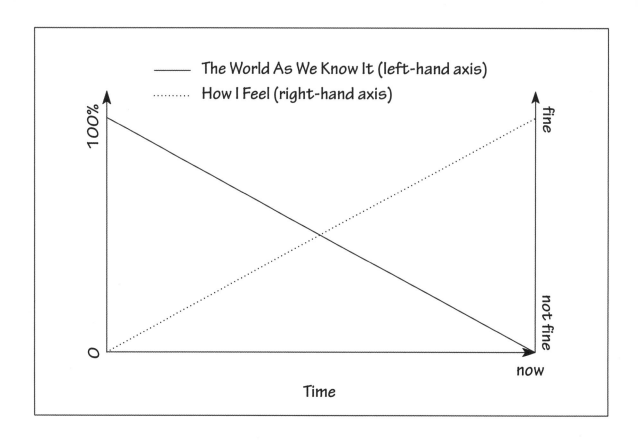

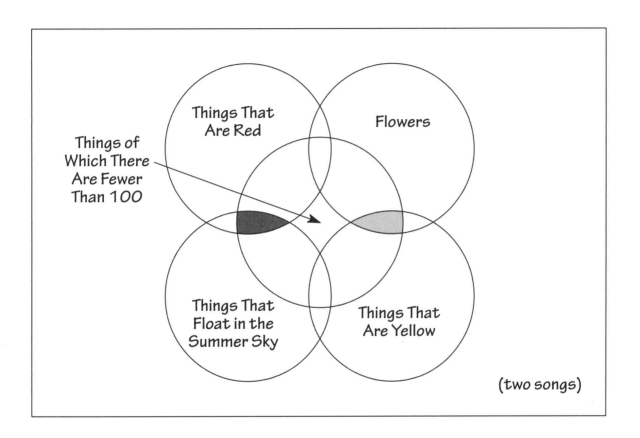

(two songs)

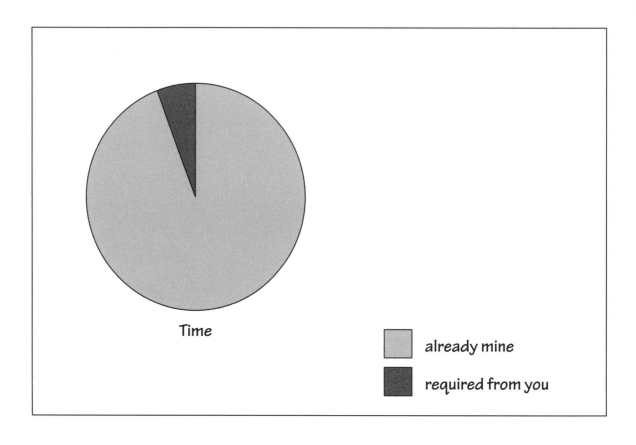

Time

already mine

required from you

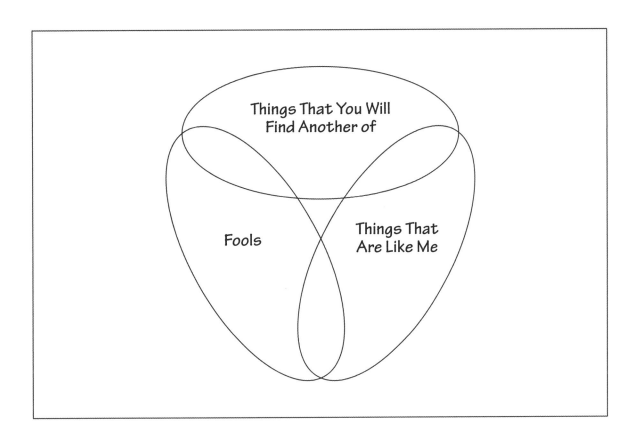

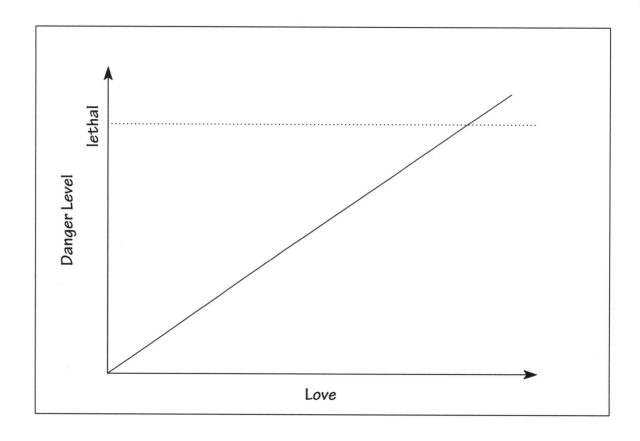

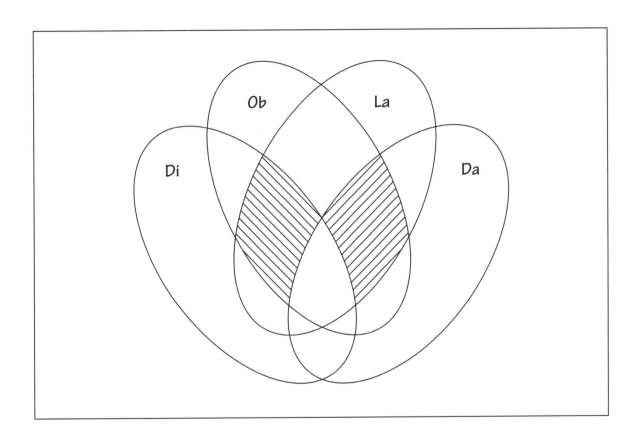

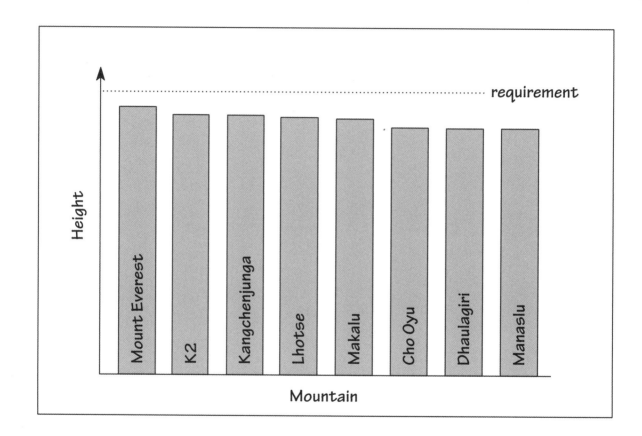

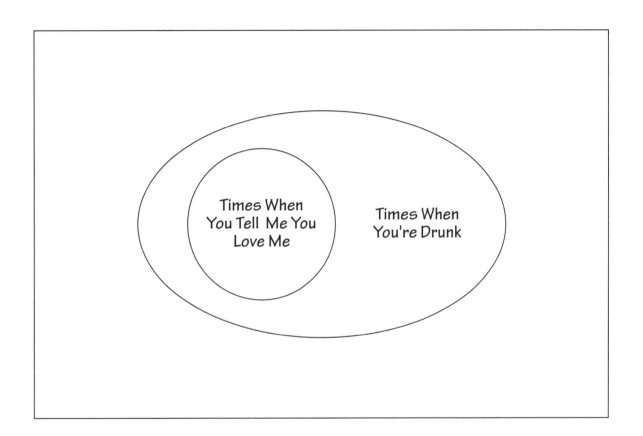

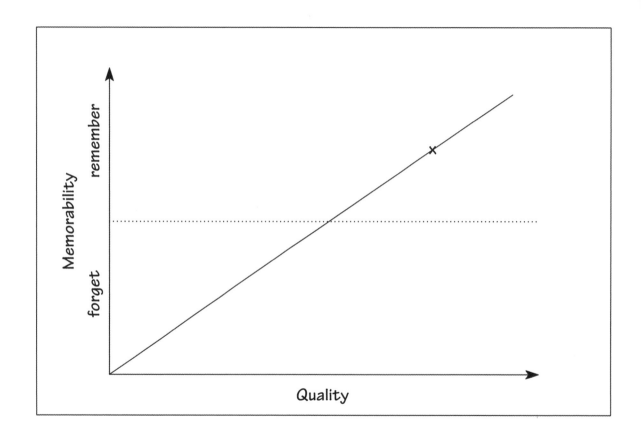

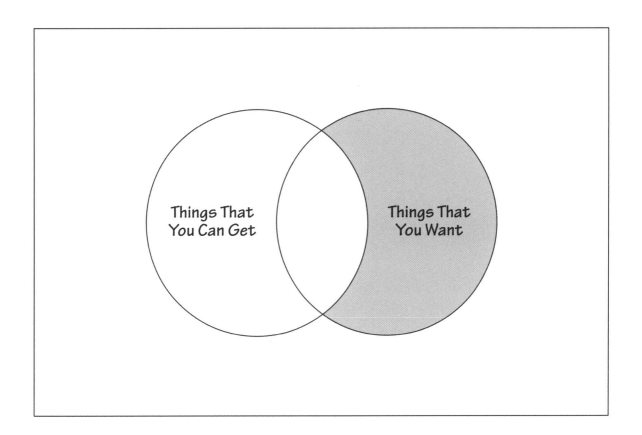

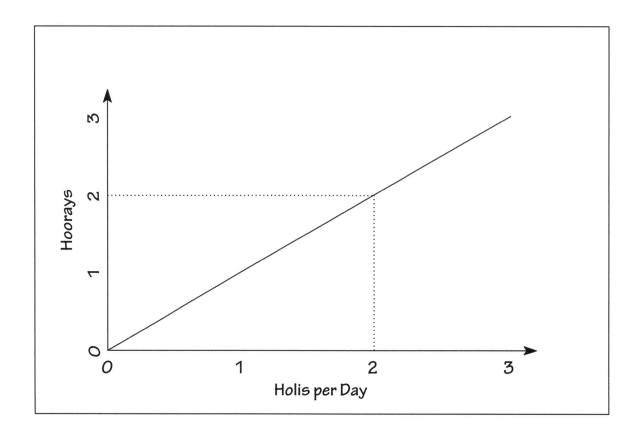

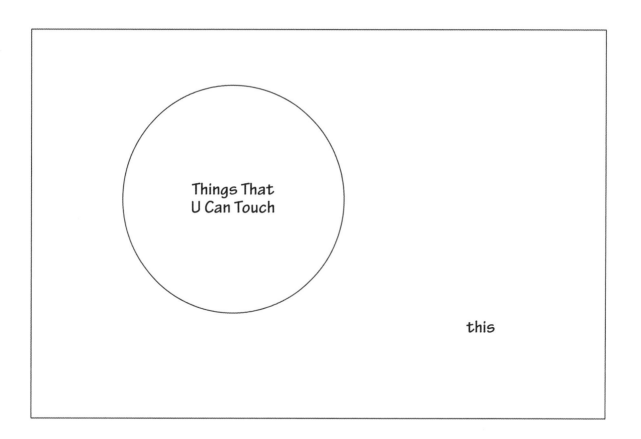

Things That
U Can Touch

this

83

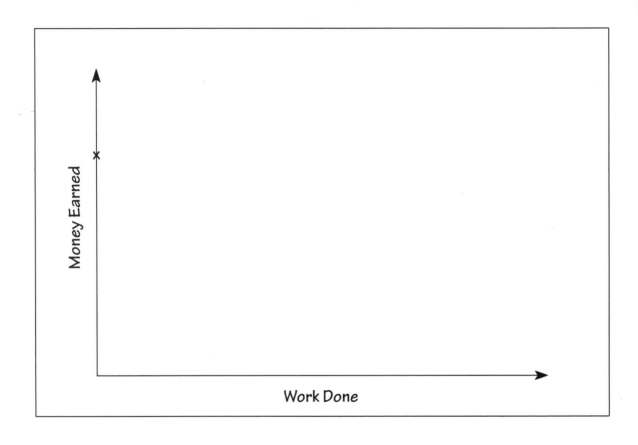

Money Earned

Work Done

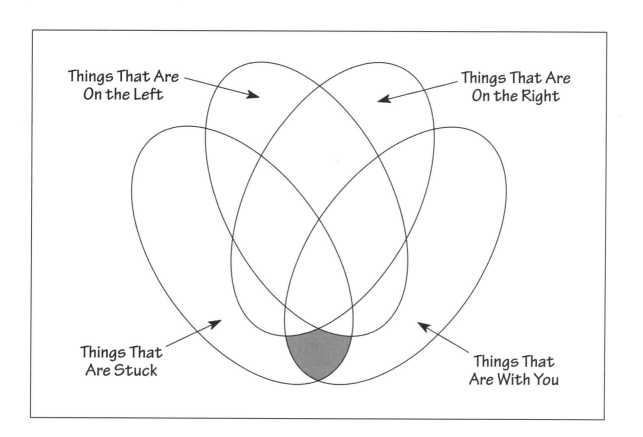

Things That Are
On the Left

Things That Are
On the Right

Things That
Are Stuck

Things That
Are With You

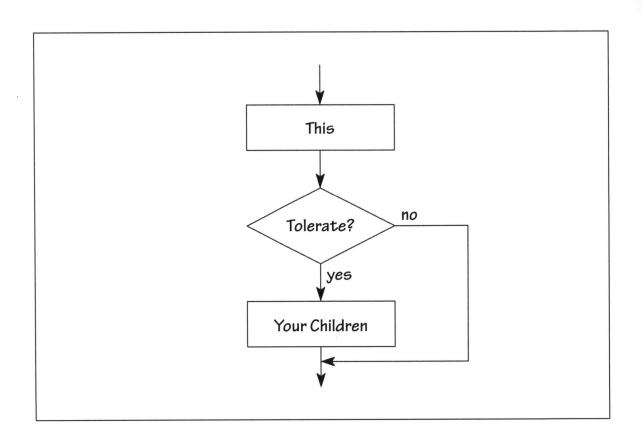

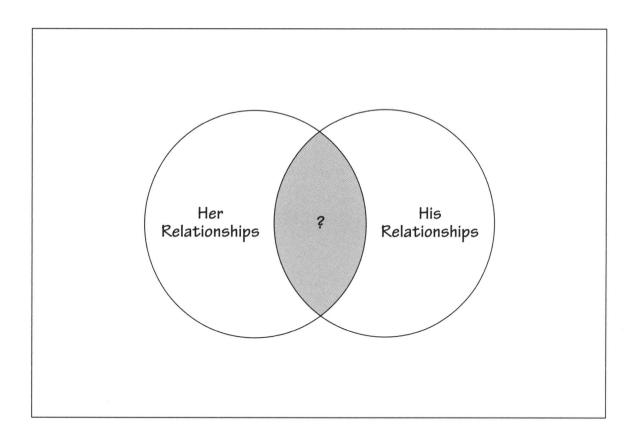

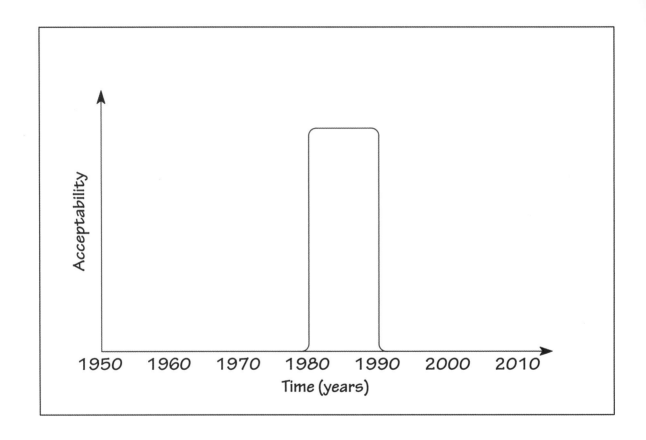

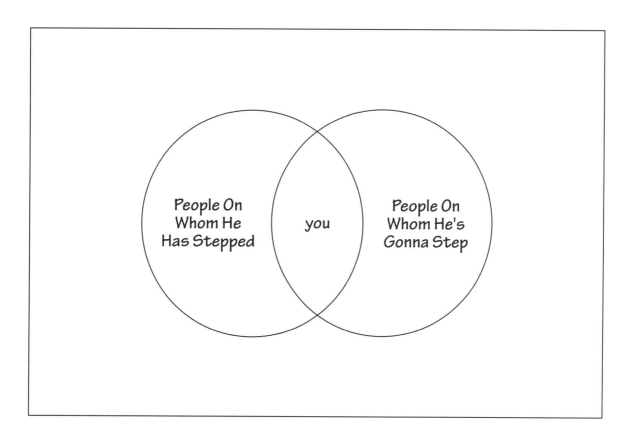

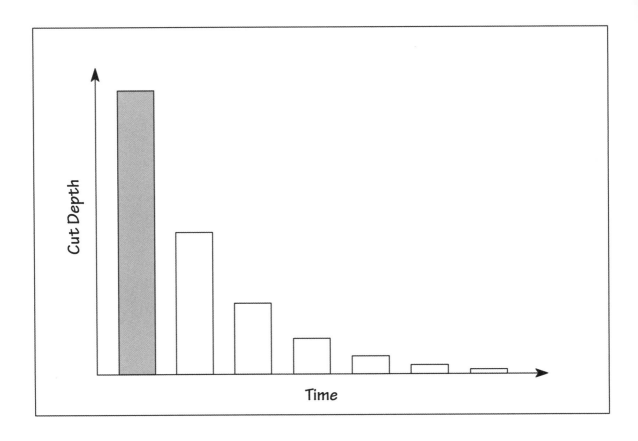

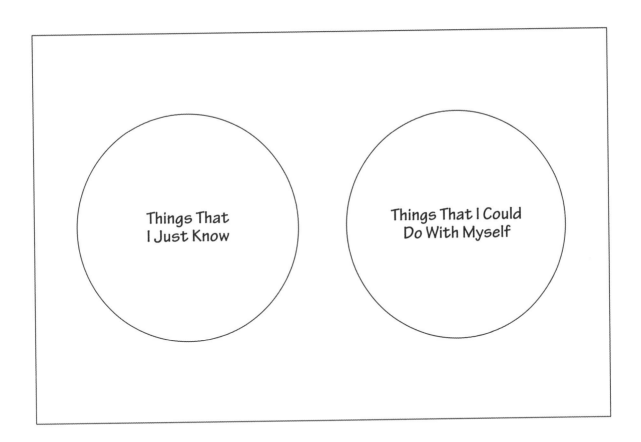

Things That
I Just Know

Things That I Could
Do With Myself

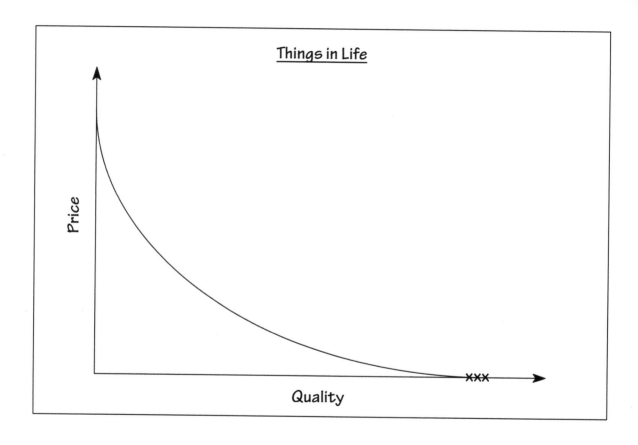

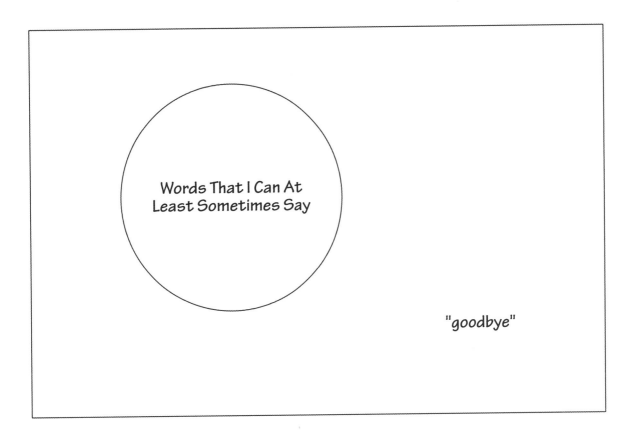

Words That I Can At
Least Sometimes Say

"goodbye"

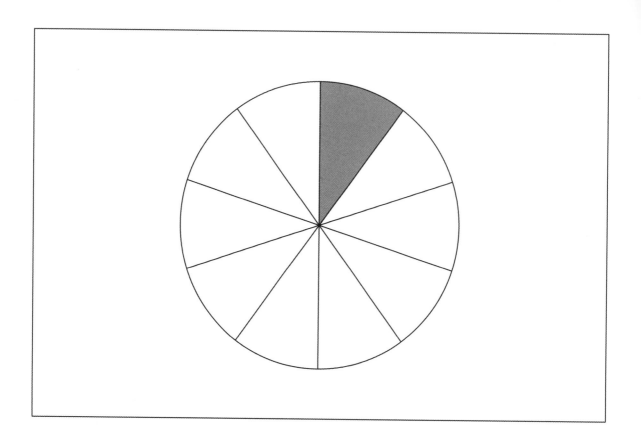

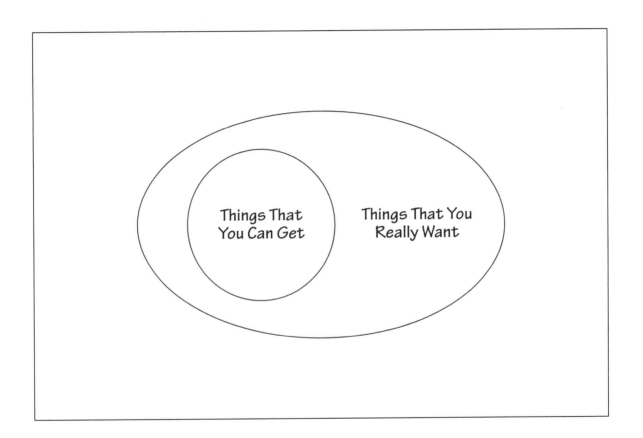

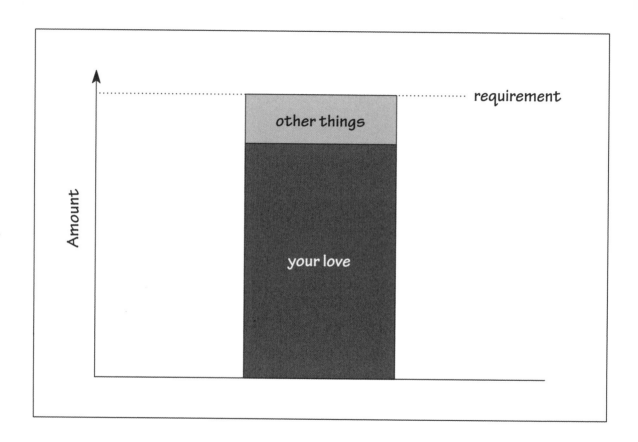

Things That You Have Not Seen So Far

Ø

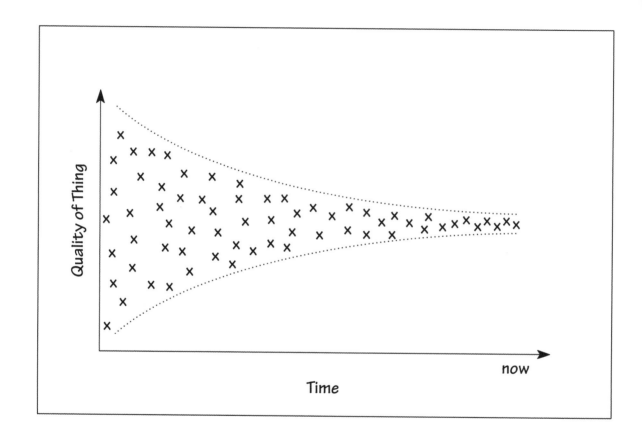

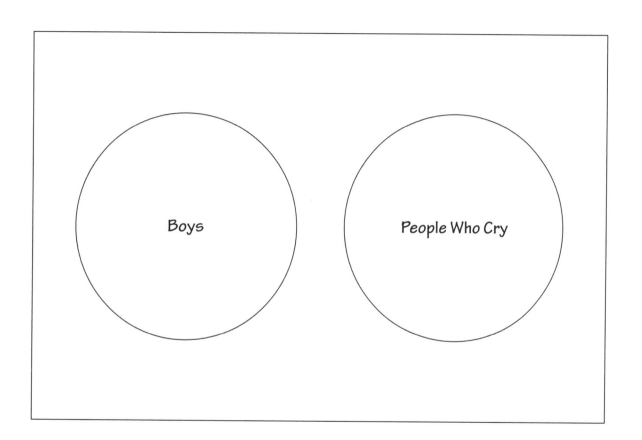

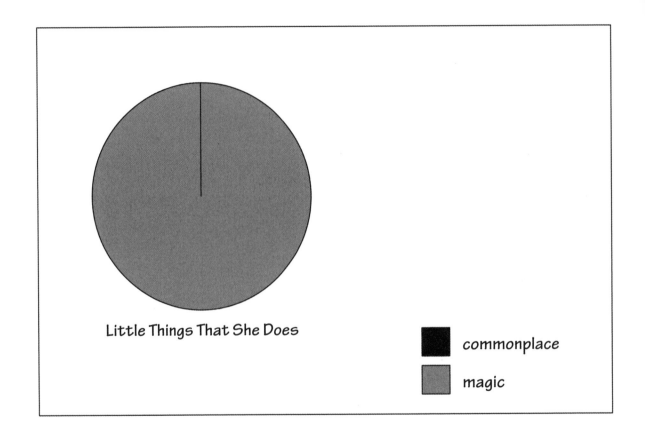

Little Things That She Does

commonplace

magic

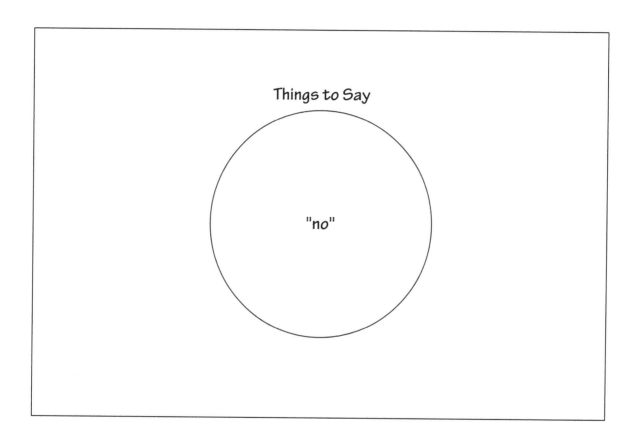

Things to Say

"no"

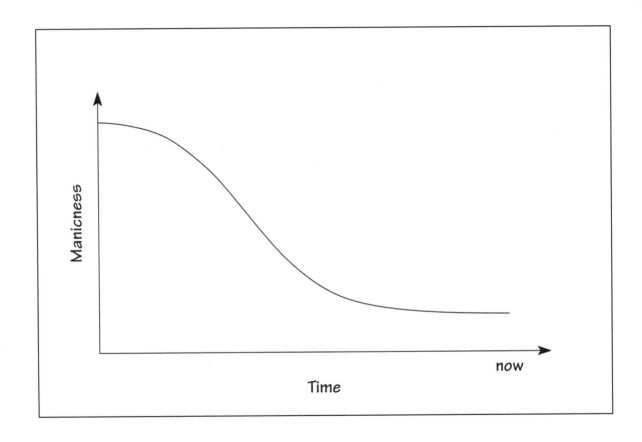

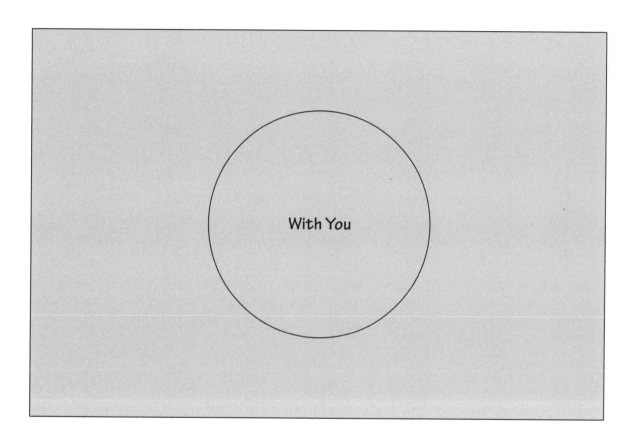

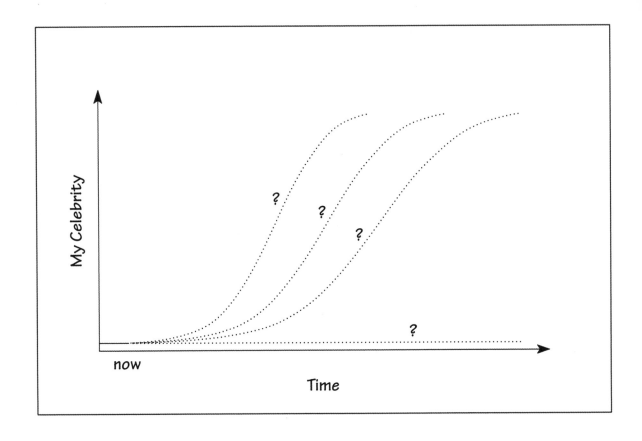

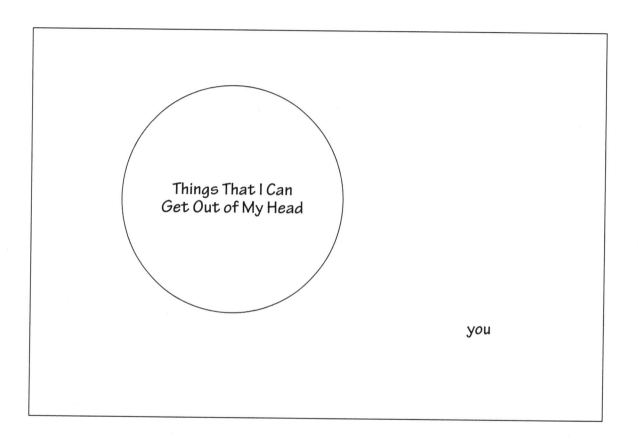

Things That I Can
Get Out of My Head

you

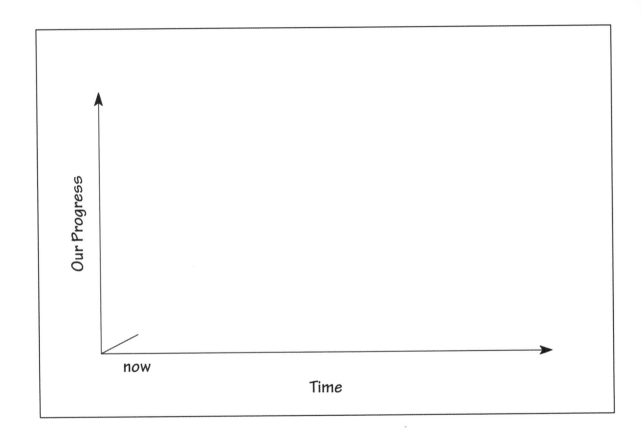

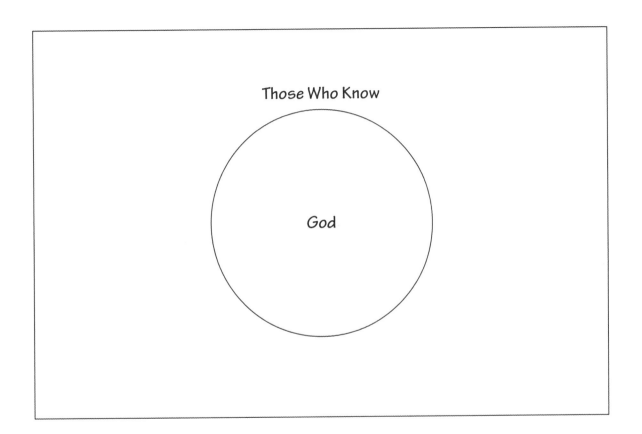

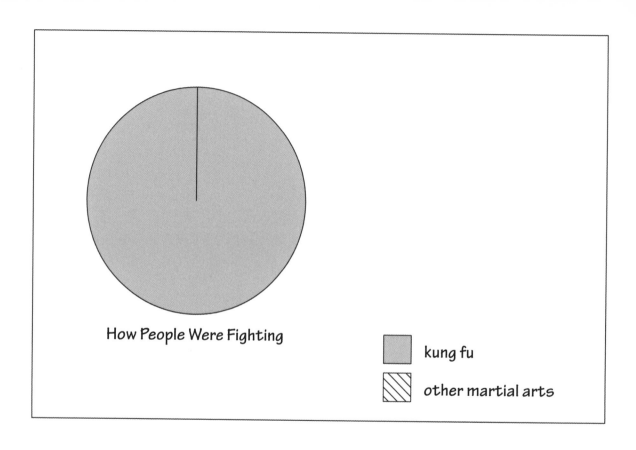

How People Were Fighting

kung fu

other martial arts

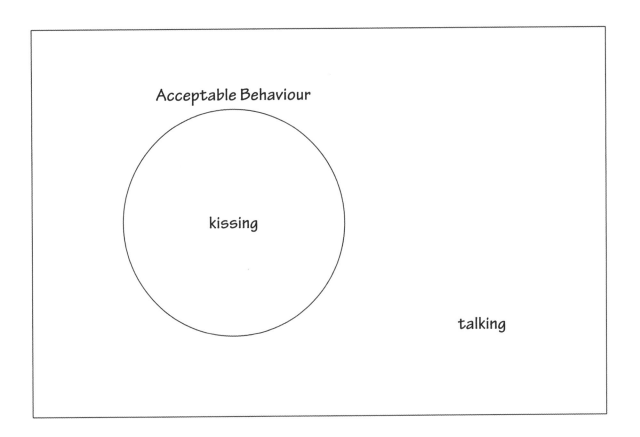

Acceptable Behaviour

kissing

talking

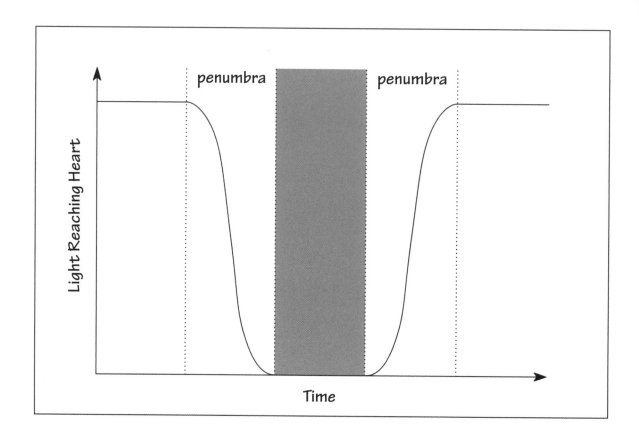

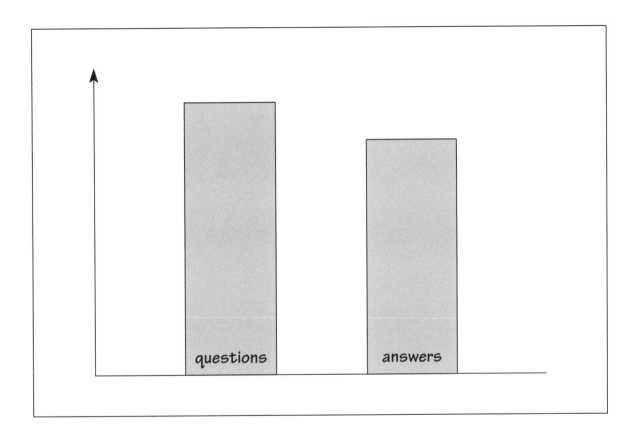

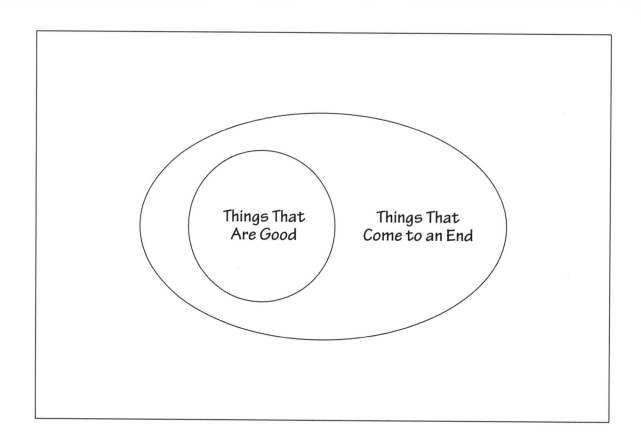

That's all there is room for. I had wanted to finish with a single by the Faces called You Can Make Me Dance, Sing Or Anything (Even Take the Dog for A Walk, Mend a Fuse, Fold Away the Ironing Board, Or Any Other Domestic Shortcomings), but my computer ran out of circles. Why not try drawing your own, or see more at vennthattune.com, where you can find out more about Venn diagrams.

Acknowledgements

I'd like to thank everyone at Hodder & Stoughton, my agent Simon Trewin, Dr Nick Gilbert at Heriot-Watt University for checking my maths – any remaining errors are mine, Zoe Margolis, Alex Marsh, everyone at Hutch Tours, and everyone who liked the original diagrams and asked me to do more – I hope you liked these as well.

Answers and UK Top 40 singles chart positions:

1. **I Saw Mommy Kissing Santa Claus** – The Beverley Sisters (No. 11 – Nov 1953, No. 6 – Dec 1953), Jimmy Boyd (No. 3 – Dec 1953), Billy Cotton and His Band (No. 11 – Dec 1953).

2. **When the Going Gets Tough, the Tough Get Going** – Billy Ocean (No. 1 – Feb 1986); **When the Going Gets Tough** – Boyzone (No. 1 – Mar 1999).

3. **Where the Streets Have No Name** – U2 (No. 4 – Sep 1987); re-recorded as **Where the Streets Have No Name (I Can't Take My Eyes Off You)** by Pet Shop Boys (No. 4 – Mar 1991).

4. **It Ain't What You Do It's the Way That You Do It** – Fun Boy Three and Bananarama (No. 4 – Mar 1982); **Ain't What You Do** – Big Brovaz (No. 15 – Dec 2003). Originally recorded by Jimmy Lunceford and His Orchestra as **T'ain't What You Do** (1939).

5. **Annie, I'm Not Your Daddy** – Kid Creole and the Coconuts (No. 2 – Oct 1982).

6. **Things Can Only Get Better** – Howard Jones (No. 6 – Feb 1985), D:Ream (No. 24 – Feb 1993, No. 1 – Jan 1994, No. 19 – May 1997).

7. **We Don't Need Another Hero (Thunderdome)** – Tina Turner (No. 3 – Aug 1985). Or perhaps the left-hand set could be "Things That Billy Should Be" – Paper Lace (No. 1 – Mar 1974).

8. **This Town Ain't Big Enough for Both of Us** – Sparks (No. 2 – Jun 1974), Sparks vs Faith No More (No. 40 – Dec 1997), British Whale (No. 6 – Aug 2005).

9. **Gimme All Your Lovin'** – ZZ Top (No. 10 – Nov 1984), Jocelyn Brown and Kym Mazelle (No. 22 – Oct 1994); **Gimme All Your Lovin' 2000** – Martay featuring ZZ Top (No. 28 – Oct 1999). The Spencer Davis Group only required "some" lovin' (No. 2 – Nov 1966), as did Thunder (No. 36 – Jul 1990). In this case there would be an intersection between the two sets, but one would not necessarily be a

subset of the other (though it could be argued that "some" lovin' could still be all of "your" lovin').

10. **Save Your Kisses For Me** – Brotherhood of Man (No. 1 – Mar 1976).

11. **(How Much Is) That Doggie in the Window?** – Patti Page (No. 9 – Mar 1953), Lita Roza (No. 1 – Apr 1953). An extra intersection could be with the set "Things With Waggly Tails".

12. **I Fought the Law** – The Bobby Fuller Four (No. 33 – Apr 1966), The Clash (No. 22 – Jun 1979 as part of The Cost of Living EP, No. 29 – Mar 1988). Originally recorded by The Crickets (1961). "I fought the law and the law won". This diagram is a matrix used in the mathematical branch of game theory. The Nash Equilibrium is derived from the fact that Me's best strategy is always to fight; The Law knows this so will always fight as well. And looking at the reward values (-10 for Me, 3 for The Law) The Law wins every time. This is despite the fact that it is better for both (-5 and 5 respectively) if neither fight. This counter-intuitive outcome can also be seen in other game theory examples such as both sides stockpiling weapons in an arms race. Though I Came Quietly (and Got Six Months Off for Good Behaviour) is also a bit less rock'n'roll.

13. **Don't You (Forget About Me)** – Simple Minds (No. 7 – May 1985).

14. **You Get What You Give** – New Radicals (No. 5 – Apr 1999), LMC featuring Rachel McFarlane (No. 30 – Feb 2006).

15. **Itsy Bitsy Teenie Weenie Yellow Polkadot Bikini** – Brian Hyland (No. 8 – Aug 1960); **Itsy Bitsy Teeny Weeny Yellow Polka Dot Bikini** – Bombalurina (No. 1 – Aug 1990).

16. **I Bet You Look Good On the Dancefloor** – Arctic Monkeys (No. 1 – Oct 2005).

17. **All I Want for Christmas Is You** – Mariah Carey (No. 2 – Dec 1994, No. 4 – Dec 2007). Dora Bryan only wanted a Beatle (No. 20 – Dec 1963), Half Man Half Biscuit only wanted a Dukla Prague Away Kit (B-side to **The Trumpton Riots**, No. 82 – Mar 1986) and Spike Jones only wanted his two front teeth (US No. 1 – Jan 1949).

18. **Instant Karma! (We All Shine On)** – John Ono Lennon (No. 5 – Feb 1970).

19. **What Have I Done to Deserve This?** – Pet Shop Boys with Dusty Springfield (No. 2 – Aug 1987).

20. **Everybody Wants to Rule the World** – Tears For Fears (No. 2 – Apr 1985). Though a year later everybody wanted to run it (No. 5 – Jun 1986).

21. **I Love to Love (But My Baby Loves to Dance)** – Tina Charles (No. 1 – Mar 1976).

22. **Eternal Flame** – The Bangles (No. 1 – Apr 1989), Atomic Kitten (No. 1 – Aug 2001). Or possibly **There Is a Light That Never Goes Out** – The Smiths (No. 25 – Oct 1992), Morrissey (No. 11 – Apr 2005).

23. **The Only Way Is Up** – Yazz and the Plastic Population (No. 1 – Aug 1988).

24. **The Power of Love** – Frankie Goes to Hollywood (No. 1 – Dec 1984, No. 10 – Dec 1993, No. 6 – Jul 2000), Huey Lewis and the News (No. 11 – Sep 1985, No. 9 – Mar 1986), Jennifer Rush (No. 1 – Oct 1985), Deee-Lite (No. 25 – Dec 1990), Celine Dion (No. 4 – Feb 1994); **Power of Love/Love Power** – Luther Vandross (No. 31 – Nov 1995). Power equals work done divided by time taken, which is the slope of this graph at any particular point. Well, how else would one measure the power of love? (Use of skyscraping doves not allowed.)

25. **He Ain't Heavy, He's My Brother** – The Hollies (No. 3 – Nov 1969, No. 1 – Sep 1988), Bill Medley (No. 25 – Sep 1988).

26. **The Winner Takes It All** – Abba (No. 1 – Aug 1980).

27. **Should I Stay Or Should I Go** – The Clash (No. 17 – Oct 1982, No. 1 – Mar 1991). Further options are "cool it" and "blow". There is also scope for a bar chart illustrating the amount of trouble that there will be for going compared with that for staying.

28. **Everyday Is Like Sunday** – Morrissey (No. 9 – Jun 1988).

29. **John, I'm Only Dancing** – David Bowie (No. 12 – Oct 1972, No. 12 – Jan 1980 (Again)), The Polecats (No. 35 – Apr 1981).

30. **Too Much Too Young** – The Specials (No. 1 – Feb 1980 as part of The Special AKA Live! EP), Little Angels (No. 22 – Nov 1992).
31. **Everyday Is a Winding Road** – Sheryl Crow (No. 12 – Nov 1996).
32. **Saving All My Love for You** – Whitney Houston (No. 1 – Dec 1985). Originally recorded by Marilyn McCoo and Billy Davis Jr (1978).
33. **Do They Know It's Christmas?** – Band Aid (No. 1 – Dec 1984, No. 3 – Dec 1985, No. 24 – Dec 2007), Band Aid II (No. 1 – Dec 1989), Band Aid 20 (No. 1 – Dec 2004).
34. **Wherever I Lay My Hat (That's My Home)** – Paul Young (No. 1 – Jul 1983). This function is bijective as it is both injective (a hat laid in a different place is a different home) and surjective (all of my homes are places where I have laid my hat).
35. **I Don't Want to Talk About It** – Rod Stewart (No. 1 – May 1977), Everything But the Girl (No. 3 – Jul 1988). Or possibly **Won't Talk About It** – Beats International (No. 9 – May 1990).
36. **Nice Legs Shame About Her Face** – The Monks (No. 19 – May 1979).
37. **It Isn't, It Wasn't, It Ain't Never Gonna Be** – Aretha Franklin and Whitney Houston (No. 29 – Sep 1989).
38. **The More You Ignore Me, the Closer I Get** – Morrissey (No. 8 – Mar 1994).
39. **(Everything I Do) I Do It for You** – Bryan Adams (No. 1 – Jul 1991), Fatima Mansions (No. 7 – Sep 1992). A question arises over whether "Things That I Do" is a proper or improper subset of "Things That Are Done for You" (ie does "Things That Are Done for You" contain anything other than "Things That I Do"?) A (mercifully) quick listen reveals that "No other could give more love", implying that others are at least trying to do things for you, therefore almost certainly making "Things That I Do" a proper subset.
40. **A Little Less Conversation** – Elvis vs JXL (No. 1 – Jun 2002, No. 3 – May 2005). "A little less conversation, a little more action."
41. **What's Love Got to Do With It** – Tina Turner (No. 3 – Aug 1984), Warren G featuring Adina Howard

(No. 2 – Nov 1996).

42. **Everyday I Love You Less and Less** – Kaiser Chiefs (No. 10 – May 2005).

43. **Ain't Gonna Bump No More (With No Big Fat Woman)** – Joe Tex (No. 2 – May 1977).

44. **Love Plus One** – Haircut 100 (No. 3 – Mar 1982).

45. **All You Need Is Love** – The Beatles (No. 1 – Jul 1967), Tom Jones (No. 19 – Feb 1993).

46. **Losing My Religion** – REM (No. 19 – Mar 1991).

47. **You're the First, the Last, My Everything** – Barry White (No. 1 – Dec 1974), Howard Brown (No. 13 – Mar 2005).

48. **You'll Never Walk Alone** – Gerry and the Pacemakers (No. 1 – Nov 1963), The Crowd (No. 1 – Jun 1985), Robson and Jerome (No. 1 – Nov 1996), The Three Tenors (No. 21 – Jul 1998). Originally from the Rodgers and Hammerstein musical *Carousel* (1945). The shaded area and solid line show that you will always have at least one walking companion.

49. **Every Loser Wins** – Nick Berry (No. 1 – Oct 1986).

50. **Can't Get Enough of Your Love, Babe** – Barry White (No. 8 – Sep 1974). This supply and demand curve shows demand of your love, babe exceeding supply of your love, babe.

51. **You Spin Me Round (Like a Record)** – Dead or Alive (No. 1 – Mar 1985); re-released as **You Spin Me Round** (No. 23 – May 2003, No. 5 – Feb 2006).

52. **Uptown Top Ranking** – Althea and Donna (No. 1 – Feb 1978), Ali and Frazier (No. 33 – Aug 1993).

53. **Ever Fallen in Love (With Someone You Shouldn't've)?** – Buzzcocks (No. 12 – Nov 1978), Various Artists as a tribute to John Peel (No. 28 – Dec 2005); re-recorded as **Ever Fallen in Love?** – Fine Young Cannibals (No. 9 – Apr 1987).

54. **Better the Devil You Know** – Kylie Minogue (No. 2 – May 1990), Sonia (No. 15 – May 1993), Steps (No. 4 – Jan 2000).

55. **Papa's Got a Brand New Bag** – James Brown and the Famous Flames (No. 25 – Oct 1965). Or possibly, if a pigbag is a type of bag, **Papa's Got a Brand New Pigbag** – Pigbag (No. 3 – Apr 1982).
56. **There's No One Quite Like Grandma** – St Winifred's School Choir (No. 1 – Dec 1980).
57. **I'd Do Anything for Love (But I Won't Do That)** – Meat Loaf (No. 1 – Oct 1993).
58. **Mama Weer All Crazee Now** – Slade (No. 1 – Sep 1972).
59. **I Started Something I Couldn't Finish** – The Smiths (No. 23 – Nov 1987).
60. **It's 'Orrible Being in Love (When You're 8½)** – Claire and Friends (No. 13 – Jul 1986).
61. **Games Without Frontiers** – Peter Gabriel (No. 4 – Mar 1980).
62. **Money's Too Tight (to Mention)** – Simply Red (No. 13 – Jul 1985). Originally recorded by The Valentine Brothers (No. 73 – Apr 1983).
63. **Somewhere Only We Know** – Keane (No. 3 – Feb 2004).
64. **Some Guys Have All the Luck** – Robert Palmer (No. 16 – Mar 1982), Rod Stewart (No. 15 – Sep 1984), Maxi Priest (No. 12 – Nov 1987). Originally a US hit for the Persuaders (No. 39 – 1973).
65. **Signed, Sealed, Delivered I'm Yours** – Stevie Wonder (No. 15 – Aug 1970), Blue featuring Stevie Wonder and Angie Stone (No. 11 – Dec 2003).
66. **Sorry Seems to Be the Hardest Word** – Elton John (No. 11 – Dec 1976), Blue featuring Elton John (No. 1 – Dec 2002, No. 36 Mar 2003). There is some dispute about the saddest word though: Celine Dion thought that it was "Goodbye" (No. 38 – Dec 2002), whilst The Stylistics claimed that it was "Na Na" (No. 5 – Dec 1975).
67. **Anyone Can Fall in Love** – Anita Dobson and the Simon May Orchestra (No. 4 – Aug 1986). All people are in the first set, so, because the sets are disjoint, the second set must be empty.
68. **Whatever Will Be, Will Be (Qué Será, Será)** – Doris Day (No. 1 – Aug 1956).
69. **Love Don't Live Here Anymore** – Rose Royce (No. 2 – Oct 1978), Jimmy Nail (No. 3 – May 1985),

Double Trouble (No. 21 – Jul 1990).

70. **Everybody Needs Somebody to Love** – The Blues Brothers (No. 12 – Apr 1990). This function is non-injective (not everybody needs to love a different person) and non-surjective (not everybody needs to be loved by somebody). For world happiness one would require a bijective function: Everybody Needs One Person of Their Own to Love and to Be Loved in Return By That Person. This would require an even number of people.

71. **What Have You Done for Me Lately** – Janet Jackson (No. 3 – May 1986).

72. **It's the End of the World As We Know It (and I Feel Fine)** – REM (No. 39 – Dec 1991).

73. **99 Red Balloons** – Nena (No. 1 – Mar 1984); **Eighteen Yellow Roses** – Bobby Darin (No. 37 – Aug 1963). So, where would **Ten Green Bottles** go?

74. **Give Me Just a Little More Time** – Chairmen of the Board (No. 3 – Sep 1970), Kylie Minogue (No. 2 – Feb 1992).

75. **You Won't Find Another Fool Like Me** – The New Seekers (No. 1 – Jan 1974).

76. **Too Much Love Will Kill You** – Brian May (No. 5 – Sep 1992), Queen (No. 15 – Mar 1996).

77. **Ob-La-Di Ob-La-Da** – Marmalade (No. 1 – Jan 1969), Bedrocks (No. 20 – Jan 1969). Originally recorded by The Beatles (1968).

78. **Ain't No Mountain High Enough** – Diana Ross (No. 6 – Oct 1970), Jocelyn Brown (No. 35 – Aug 1998).

79. **You Only Tell Me You Love Me When You're Drunk** – Pet Shop Boys (No. 8 – Jan 2000).

80. **Too Good to Be Forgotten** – The Chi-Lites (No. 10 – Nov 1974), Amazulu (No. 5 – Jun 1986).

81. **You Can't Always Get What You Want** – The Rolling Stones (B-side to **Honky Tonk Women**, No. 1 – Jul 1969).

82. **Hooray! Hooray! It's a Holi-Holiday** – Boney M (No. 3 – May 1979); re-recorded as **Hooray Hooray (It's a Cheeky Holiday)** by The Cheeky Girls (No. 3 – Aug 2003).

83. **U Can't Touch This** – MC Hammer (No. 3 – Aug 1990), Crazy Frog (No. 5 – Dec 2005).
84. **Money for Nothing** – Dire Straits (No. 4 – Aug 1985).
85. **Stuck in the Middle With You** – Stealer's Wheel (No. 8 – Jun 1973). So, where do the clowns and jokers go?
86. **If You Tolerate This Your Children Will Be Next** – Manic Street Preachers (No. 1 – Sep 1998).
87. **Is She Really Going Out With Him?** – Joe Jackson (No. 13 – Aug 1979).
88. **Acceptable in the 80s** – Calvin Harris (No. 10 – Mar 2007, No. 38 – Jun 2007).
89. **He's Gonna Step On You Again** – John Kongos (No. 4 – Jul 1971); re-recorded as **Step On** by Happy Mondays (No. 5 – Apr 1990).
90. **First Cut Is the Deepest** – Rod Stewart (No. 1 – May 1977); **The First Cut Is the Deepest** – PP Arnold (No. 18 – Jun 1967), Sheryl Crow (No. 37 – Nov 2003).
91. **I Just Don't Know What to Do With Myself** – Dusty Springfield (No. 3 – Jul 1964), The White Stripes (No. 13 – Sep 2003).
92. **The Best Things in Life Are Free** – Luther Vandross and Janet Jackson with special guests BBD and Ralph Tresvant (No. 2 – Aug 1992), Luther Vandross and Janet Jackson (No. 7 – Dec 1995).
93. **Never Can Say Goodbye** – The Jackson Five (No. 33 – Aug 1971), Gloria Gaynor (No. 2 – Jan 1975), The Communards (No. 4 – Nov 1987).
94. **One in Ten** – UB40 (No. 7 – Sep 1981), 808 State vs UB40 (No. 17 – Dec 1992).
95. **You Can Get It If You Really Want** – Desmond Dekker (No. 2 – Oct 1970). Perhaps the Rolling Stones didn't *really* want what they couldn't always get.
96. **Your Love Alone Is Not Enough** – Manic Street Preachers (No. 2 – May 2007).
97. **You Ain't Seen Nothing Yet** – Bachman-Turner Overdrive (No. 2 – Dec 1974); **You Ain't Seen Nothin' Yet** – Bus Stop featuring Randy Bachman (No. 22 – Oct 1998). Ø denotes the empty set, though the double negative is admittedly somewhat confusing.

98. **Everything Is Average Nowadays** – Kaiser Chiefs (No. 19 – Jun 2007).

99. **Boys Don't Cry** – The Cure (No. 22 – May 1986). Other people who don't cry are Big Girls (The Four Seasons (No. 13 – Feb 1963), Fergie (No. 2 – Jul 2007), Damned (Visage (No. 11 – Apr 1982)) and Big Boys (Lolly (No. 10 – Dec 1999)).

100. **Every Little Thing She Does Is Magic** – The Police (No. 1 – Nov 1981).

101. **Just Say No** – Grange Hill Cast (No. 5 – Apr 1986).

102. **Not So Manic Now** – Dubstar (No. 18 – Jan 1996).

103. **With Or Without You** – U2 (No. 4 – Mar 1987). The shaded area outside the circle is the complement of the area inside, and is usually denoted with a '. So, putting them together, Bono can't live (with you) or (with you)'.

104. **When Will I Be Famous?** – Bros (No. 2 – Feb 1988).

105. **Can't Get You Out of My Head** – Kylie Minogue (No. 1 – Sep 2001, No. 36 – Mar 2002).

106. **We've Only Just Begun** – The Carpenters (No. 28 – Feb 1971), Bitty McLean (No. 23 – Jun 1995).

107. **God Only Knows** – The Beach Boys (No. 2 – Aug 1966).

108. **Kung Fu Fighting** – Carl Douglas (No. 1 – Sep 1974), Bus Stop featuring Carl Douglas (No. 8 – Jun 1998). "Everybody was kung fu fighting."

109. **Don't Talk Just Kiss** – Right Said Fred with Jocelyn Brown (No. 3 – Jan 1992). Elvis vs JXL wanted less conversation and more action, but didn't specify an outright ban on the spoken word.

110. **Total Eclipse of the Heart** – Bonnie Tyler (No. 1 – Mar 1983), Nicki French (No. 5 – Feb 1995), Jan Wayne (No. 28 – Mar 2003).

111. **There Are More Questions Than Answers** – Johnny Nash (No. 9 – Oct 1972). Not here there aren't, Johnny.

112. **All Good Things (Come to an End)** – Nelly Furtado (No. 4 – Dec 2006).